FROM RED LETTER CHALLENGE

BEING

CHALLENGE

A 40-DAY CHALLENGE TO BE LIKE JESUS

ZACH ZEHNDER

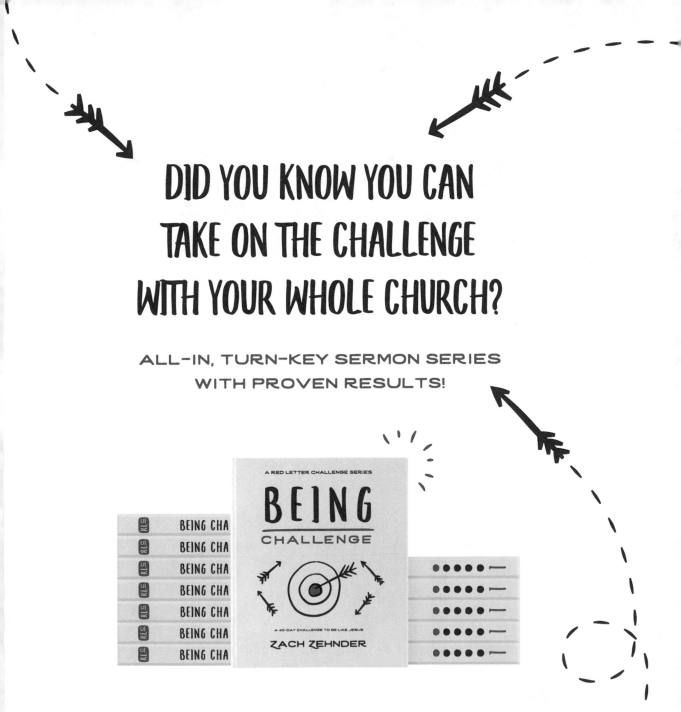

TABLE OF
CONT

ENTS

INTRO

A 40-DAY CHALLENGE TO BE LIKE JESUS

People need clear targets.

Nobody on the planet knows this truth better than Matthew Emmons. He was an American sharpshooter in the 2004 Athens Olympics—and he was, far and away, the best sharpshooter in the world.

In fact, some experts say he's the best shooter who has ever lived. That year the question wasn't who is going to win the gold, but who would take the silver and the bronze. Everyone knew Matthew Emmons was going to win the gold.

Rifle marksmen are trained to fire between heartbeats. They try to slow their heartbeat down as much as possible, sense the rhythm, and fire between beats. Olympic medals are won by millimeters, so the slightest movement is a problem. Going into his final shot, Emmons was in first place by a mile, and all he needed to do to win the gold was hit the target—anywhere on the target. It's a sport where top competitors are expected to be so accurate that we have a hard time believing they could ever miss.

With one bullet left to shoot, Emmons needed a score of 7.2 to win his second gold medal of the Olympic Games. On his first nine shots in the finals, Emmons' lowest score was a 9.3. He took careful aim, fired, and sure enough, bull's eye for the American. He did it. What else would you expect from the world's most accurate sharpshooter?

Except for one small fact: He actually shot at the wrong target, one lane over. The mistake is known as a "crossfire," and he got a score of 0. Those of us who have gone bowling and somehow skipped over our lane and rolled a strike in the next lane may know the feeling. It's impressive, but it doesn't count for anything!

In a press conference after the event, Emmons said he felt great going into his last shot. He explained that he was more concerned with calming himself than looking at his target. He dropped from first to eighth and didn't medal.

Why do I bring this up? Because Matthew Emmons, who was literally the greatest shooter in the world, teaches us that if you focus on the wrong thing, you won't hit the right target.

As Christians, we can have the best intentions in the world, but if we are succeeding at things that don't actually matter, we can do more harm than good. Really? More harm than good? Yes, it's true. D.L. Moody once said, "Our greatest fear shouldn't be of failure but at succeeding at something that doesn't matter." I'll go a step further and say my greatest fear is that Christians succeed at something that actually pushes people away from Jesus.

We've been called to represent Jesus Christ, and yet Christians are too often known for words and actions that are the opposite of Jesus' life. In their book, *UnChristian,* authors David Kinnaman and Gabe Lyons report a poll of unchurched Americans that asked them what words they associate with Christians. At the top of the list are these: judgmental, hypocritical, too political, anti-gay, out of touch, old-fashioned, and boring.[1] We may want to argue with Kinnamon or the people who participated in the poll, but those are the targets we've hit—which tells me clearly that we've been shooting at the wrong targets.

To change the narrative and to become more like Jesus, it's time to shoot at the right targets.

What are the right targets for a disciple of Jesus?

I remember a time early in my church ministry that I really wrestled with this question. I had just completed my seminary education in St. Louis, Missouri, and was called to plant a church in a suburb outside of Orlando, Florida, called Mount Dora. It was a job that was way over my head, a job that I didn't feel ready for, and truthfully, the first real venture in my life that required me to live by faith on a daily basis. It was difficult and exciting at the same time.

In those early years, I celebrated every time new people came to our church. But my favorite part was seeing someone who was dead in their sin not only receive the grace of Jesus Christ but also commit to following Him.

Derek was one of those people. He had a bad taste of church in his past, but he agreed to go to church with his girlfriend. After some time, he received God's forgiveness, was baptized, and committed to walking with Jesus. It was an exciting time, and there was a lot of enthusiasm for Derek among his family, his friends, and his new church family.

TO CHANGE THE NARRATIVE AND TO BECOME MORE LIKE JESUS, IT'S TIME TO SHOOT AT THE RIGHT TARGETS.

A week after his baptism, he approached me and said, "Pastor, I don't really feel like anything is different at all. I feel like I'm supposed to do something, but I don't know how to follow Jesus. So, what do I do now?" He was essentially asking me to help him identify his targets.

I believe that if you ask 100 Jesus-followers to identify their targets, you would probably get 100 different responses. Hopefully, all of them have some merit, but I'm often confused about why we have so many answers to what should be a very clear answer.

Derek asked a great question: "What do I do now?" It's a question all of us need to ask. When I was in seminary, I was taught an answer: "Nothing. You're saved by grace. You don't have to do anything."

I felt proud of this answer. It keeps the focus on Jesus and what He has done. He took care of it all at the cross.

That's absolutely the right answer when it comes to salvation, but it's not the answer Derek needed. As a new follower of Jesus, he wanted to know how to be in a deeper relationship with Him. In any relationship, people do things and say things to grow closer. It's the same in our relationship with Jesus. The starting point is all about Him. We can't earn our salvation by what we do. Jesus has done what we can't do. It's a gift. But in developing our relationship with Him, we can do something . . . actually, a lot of things. We take action, not to earn God's love and forgiveness, but out of the gratitude for what Jesus has done for us. We're motivated by the grace He has already poured out on us.

When Derek asked his question, I instantly realized my standard, seminary answer wasn't clear enough, and it bothered me for a long time. I wished I'd had a better answer, but I simply didn't. And then, as I was reading through Jesus' preaching in what's known as "The Sermon on the Mount," I found the answer I was looking for. Check it out!

> **"Everyone who hears these words of mine and puts them into practice is like a wise man who built his house on the rock. The rain came down, the streams rose, and the winds blew and beat against that house; yet it did not fall, because it had its foundation on the rock. But everyone who hears these words of mine and does not put them into practice is like a foolish man who built his house on sand. The rain came down, the streams rose, and the winds blew and beat against that house, and it fell with a great crash." Matthew 7:24-27**

In one of the most difficult to understand, counter-cultural, opinionated, sarcastic sermons that Jesus ever gave (by the way, Matthew said the crowds were amazed at His teaching), He ends the sermon by telling us that we are to be both hearers and doers of His words.

And that's when it struck me. The best way to follow Jesus is simply to follow Jesus.

It was so obvious to me at that moment. If our aim is to be like Jesus, why would we look to anyone but Jesus to find out what to do?

This idea—which is not my own, but borrowed from Jesus—was an idea God gave me. It's one of the few things in my life I believe was a clear, unmistakable message from God, and I knew beyond a shadow of a doubt that God wanted me to do something with it.

I began a seven-year process and resulted in something I never pictured myself doing—writing a book! I looked at everything Jesus said, with special attention to the things He was asking and commanding His disciples to do, and I found five main principles, or targets, that disciples of Jesus are called to shoot for.

I organized the book around these five targets and named it *Red Letter Challenge*. It covers 40 days. Each day includes what Jesus said and the challenge to do what He instructed . . . to hit the target.

Red Letter Challenge has gone far beyond where my dreams ever allowed me to go, and I believe the reason is simple: it points people back to Jesus and gives them clear targets to shoot for.

I've become convinced about something. Though all five of the targets in *Red Letter Challenge* are important, the most important target to hit as a disciple of Jesus is BEING in relationship with Him. It's at the center of it all. All the other targets flow from this one. All of our *doing* for God flows out of our *being* with Him. If we don't hit this one, we won't succeed at any of the others.

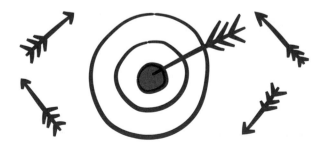

HERE ARE THE 5 TARGETS

BEING

At the heart of following Jesus is the opportunity to be in real relationship with Him. Jesus speaks a lot about different disciplines, or habits, that guide us into a deeper relationship with God.

FORGIVING

After being with Jesus, we see just how gracious our God is. Followers of Jesus are continually receiving His forgiveness, which gives them the motivation and ability to forgive others.

SERVING

After receiving forgiveness from Jesus, we can't wait to serve Him. We use our gifts and talents to serve others, believing that through our service, we can help others see Jesus.

GIVING

Jesus had a lot to say about money. The frequency of the topic and the clarity of His teaching convince me that it's impossible to be a stingy Christian. Followers of Jesus are generous!

GOING

Jesus ends all four Gospels by sending us to share the Good News with others. Jesus calls us to be His witnesses and to tell our stories of faith and forgiveness. When we combine our individual stories with the bigger story of what Jesus has done for everybody, we overcome the enemy!

Being in relationship with God:

- Helps me receive and experience His forgiveness and give it away to others.

- Reminds me of how much Jesus served me and inspires me to care for people.

- Deepens my trust that God will take care of me and provide for me so I can be generous, knowing I don't have to cling tightly to anything.

- Empowers me through the Holy Spirit to go and boldly tell others about this incredible God we follow.

Because of its importance—and frankly, our struggle simply to be in relationship with God—I wanted to explore what it looks like to develop a rich, strong connection with Him. But where do we start?

I already knew the answer to that: We start with Jesus! Remember, the best way to follow Jesus is to follow Jesus!

In *Red Letter Challenge*, I looked at the different things that Jesus called His disciples to do, and I found what I believe were the five main targets for disciples of Jesus. In *Being Challenge*, I want to focus on the ways in which Jesus himself spent time *being*, how He was in relationship with God. Think about it. If we want to grow in our relationship with God, we ought to look to the only one who was ever in perfect relationship with Him!

I read through all four Gospels in the New Testament, the books of Matthew, Mark, Luke, and John, to try and understand what Jesus' relationship with God looked like. Specifically, I was looking for the different personal and interpersonal spiritual disciplines, or habits, that Jesus practiced instead of just the outward habits that are focused on doing things. I wanted to see Jesus *be* with God. <u>What practices did Jesus put into place to be in a close relationship with God?</u>

Similar to *Red Letter Challenge*, I wanted to identify five main habits for us to put into practice. While some lists of spiritual disciplines have up to 30 different practices, I believe it's important to shoot for something we can hit. For that reason, we'll focus on five keystone habits of Jesus, which are the *Being Challenge* targets. After extensive study of the habits Jesus put into practice (you can see the methodology of the study in the appendix), I found five that Jesus regularly practiced to be in relationship with God.

COMMIT TO COMMUNITY
STUDY SCRIPTURE
PRIORITIZE PRAYER
SEEK SOLITUDE
CHOOSE CHURCH

KEYSTONE HABITS

Being Challenge explores these five habits, and how they not only informed the life of Jesus, but also, how they can help shape your life and mine. I believe that if you grow in these habits, your relationship with God will deepen, and ultimately, you will be the disciple He has called you to be.

At the end of the day, true disciples want to be the best representation of Jesus. After all that He's done for us and the grace He's given us, not only to forgive us, but to allow us to wake up each day with breath in our lungs and talents to make a difference, we want to be the best, most effective, greatest followers of Jesus on the planet! We want others to see how great our God is!

When you incorporate these five habits into your life, you'll live the abundant life that Jesus describes. You'll walk in a deep relationship with God, and you will make a big difference in the world.

The rest of this book will explore these five habits.

Our introduction will describe the importance of keystone habits.

Days 1-5 will dive into how the five keystone habits played out in the life of Jesus.

Starting on Day 6 and going through Day 40, we'll have daily devotions with challenges for you to complete:

DAYS
6-12
Commit to Community

DAYS
13-19
Study Scripture

DAYS
20-26
Prioritize Prayer

DAYS
27-33
Seek Solitude

DAYS
34-40
Choose Church

CHALLENGE RECOMMENDATIONS

1 DON'T DO THIS ALONE

Reading and acting on the words of Jesus is best done in community. Therefore, we've created some companion resources for you online at www.beingchallenge.com. There you'll find resources for using *Being Challenge* in a small group or as a church, but at a minimum, we suggest asking at least one friend to join you for this 40-day challenge.

2 GIVE YOURSELF GRACE

On some days it'll be easy for you to accomplish a challenge, but other days will be difficult. The goal isn't that you would do every day perfectly, but rather, that you would be challenged to grow in your relationship with God. Even though this is a book that's primarily about being with God, there are a lot of things I'll challenge you to do. If you fail, you may be tempted to give up—but don't! When you get discouraged, lean harder into the love, forgiveness, and power of God. Give yourself grace and keep moving. Walking with Jesus isn't a straight path. When we stumble, we're met by a God who leads us with grace and gives us another opportunity. Take it.

KEYSTONE HABITS

THE IMPORTANCE OF KEYSTONE HABITS

The introduction started with the story of an American Olympian in Athens who failed in the clutch. Now, let's move to another star, Michael Phelps, who just happens to be the greatest, most drippin' Olympian of all-time, accumulating a record 23 gold medals and 28 total medals.

Each medal is special, but I would argue that the gold medal Phelps won in the 200-meter butterfly in the 2008 Beijing Games is far and away his most impressive.

There are many reasons Phelps' excelled as a swimmer. He has the right body type—big hands, a long, powerful torso, short legs, and feet that rotate beyond ninety degrees. In fact, he can bend his feet more than most ballerinas. It's one thing to have the natural body for a sport, but Phelps also put in the work. During training, he was known for swimming nearly 50 miles in a week. That's six hours a day, six days a week! (Many of us would struggle to do six laps in a neighborhood pool.)

But it wasn't always easy for him. Early in his career, he got nervous before his races. Like many of us, the greater the challenge, the more nervous he got.

His coach helped him acquire a set of habits for his pre-race routine. Even as the competitions and challenges got bigger, the way he got ready for them was always the same.

Check out some of Phelps' habits:

- He ate a breakfast of eggs, oatmeal, and four high calorie shakes. He never varied the menu. In fact, in his days of serious training, Phelps consumed up to 12,000 calories a day! (This isn't a good habit for you and me . . . unless we're swimming six hours a day.)

- He did the same warm-ups and stretches.

- He put on his racing suit, which was so tight that it took 20 minutes to get on.

- He put on his headphones and listened to the same mix of rap-music that was on his playlist in training.

- Finally, he played an imaginary videotape in his mind that visualized every element of the upcoming race. He closed his eyes, took deep breaths, and "saw" exactly how many strokes it was going to take for him to complete the race.

After all this, Michael Phelps was ready for the starting block. I distinctly remember watching Phelps on television. He did these crazy arm swings that slapped his back. You could see the perfect swimmer's body, flexibility, and strength that made him a champion. (His arm swinging also may have been designed to intimidate other swimmers.)

So why was the 200-meter butterfly at the 2008 Olympic Games in Beijing his most impressive? After all, it was his strongest event, and he was expected to win. It's so impressive because of what happened as he dove into the water. At that moment, it was less about Phelps' ability and more about his habits that enabled him to win.

When Phelps dove into the water, his goggles were jostled and started leaking water. There was nothing he could do. A swimmer can't stop for a second to make any adjustments, especially in a short race. The problem got increasingly worse, and by the time Phelps reached the final turn, he was almost blind. He couldn't see the black line that marked the bottom of the pool or the black tee at the end of the pool. But he didn't panic.

As part of Phelps' training over the previous months, his coach had him swim in a pitch-dark pool. Now, the preparation paid off. As he made the final turn, entered his sprint, and neared the finish, the crowd was cheering wildly. But Phelps didn't know why they were cheering. Was he in the lead? Had he been overtaken by a local favorite? He was counting his strokes, knowing he had 21 strokes to finish. At this point, he was depending on the imaginary videotape in his mind.

He counted them off 19, 20, and he felt he needed a big 21st. One more big one…21…and as he reached the end of the stroke, his hand touched the edge of the pool. He ripped off his goggles and looked at the scoreboard. Beside his name

he saw the letters "WR." Not only did he win a gold medal, but blinded by water in his goggles, Michael Phelps set the world record![2]

Phelps' habits had prepared him for the big race and the big win. This story shows us the power of habits. As we do things over and over, they become easier and easier until one day, we can do them blindfolded—without even thinking about them.

Did you know that about 40% of the actions we perform each day aren't actual decisions, but habits?[3] 40%! That means almost half of what we do isn't the result of thoughtful decision-making. And while each habit may mean very little on its own, over time the meals we consume, what we say to our family and friends each day, whether we save or spend, and how often we work out have an enormous impact on our health, productivity, financial security, and happiness.

As a pastor, I have focused a lot of my attention on trying to help people make the right decisions. But if I want them to be great followers of Jesus, I need to teach them to develop the necessary habits that will automatically put them in a position to make good decisions.

40% OF THE ACTIONS WE PERFORM EACH DAY AREN'T ACTUAL DECISIONS, BUT HABITS.

So, what's a habit? The definition is "a regular tendency or practice, especially one that is hard to give up."

Why are habits important? "Habits emerge because the brain is constantly looking for ways to save effort. Left to its own devices, the brain will try to make almost any routine into a habit, because habits allow our minds to ramp down more often."[4] In other words, a good habit is one that saves time and energy so we can focus on making a good decision in another area of our lives.

So, what are your habits?

All of us have good and bad habits. Habits serve an important purpose or you wouldn't do them.

You might say, "Well, what about picking your nose in traffic?" It's a habit that most of us have. Believe it or not, a study by insurance provider NetQuote found that 66% of respondents admitted to picking while driving.[5] Even though it's frowned upon, the nose gets cleaned out and stress is taken care of. (I suppose because boogers are uncomfortable.) It serves a purpose. Seinfeld lost a girlfriend because he was wrongly accused of picking his nose at a stoplight, but most of us do it.

A more positive habit is flossing your teeth. I can't stand flossing. I hate it every time I go to the dentist and the hygienist asks me if I've been flossing regularly. I'm always tempted to lie, but I'm sure my bloody gums tell the truth. Thankfully, because of the game *Fortnight* and the Floss Dance, I can now with integrity tell my dentist I regularly floss. Flossing your teeth serves a purpose. It cleans the teeth, reduces risk of gum disease, gives you fresher breath, and over the long haul, probably saves money on dental bills.

It's a worthwhile goal to eliminate (or reduce) bad habits and instill good ones. I know, I'm a genius, right?! But it's a lifelong process.

One of the best books on habits, a New York Times best seller, is *The Power of Habit* by Charles Duhigg, who introduces us to a concept called *"keystone habits."*

The definition of a keystone habit is: "a habit that people introduce into their lives that unintentionally carries over into other aspects of their lives."[6]

KEYSTONE HABITS:

A HABIT THAT PEOPLE INTRODUCE INTO THEIR LIVES THAT UNINTENTIONALLY CARRIES OVER INTO OTHER ASPECTS OF THEIR LIVES.

#BEINGCHALLENGE

Keystone habits create a domino effect that can change every area of your life. One crucial habit leads to other good habits. A keystone habit is no more difficult to form than any other one, but it provides multiplied benefits.

Here are some examples:

1 EXERCISING REGULARLY:
Research shows that people who exercise have increased patience and less stress and are more productive at work. Consistent workouts are also correlated with good nutrition and better sleep. And crazily enough, regular exercise has also been linked to spending less on credit cards. Have you been trying to get your spouse to spend less money on credit cards? Get him or her to exercise!

2 TRACKING WHAT YOU EAT
The National Institutes of Health conducted an extensive study, dividing people who had weight loss goals into two categories: those who tracked their eating and those who didn't. They found that those who journaled and tracked their eating lost twice as much weight as those who didn't. If you want to see some success with the goals you set, keep a journal.[7]

3 MAKING YOUR BED EVERY MORNING
I know, it feels like a waste of time because you're just going to mess it up again that night, but making your bed is correlated with increased productivity. Bed makers are more likely to enjoy their jobs, own a home, exercise regularly, and feel rested. They also have a stronger ability to stick to a budget.

FLOSSING YOUR TEETH

Many of us know we should floss, but we don't want to do it. Did you know that many lifestyle coaches who start with new clients introduce flossing as the first habit to develop? Why? You're starting with an achievable goal that produces the subconscious message: "I'm a disciplined person. I will choose what's right over what I want to do or what's easy." That's a powerful message that carries over into other areas of life. Flossing is associated with successful, capable, confident, and disciplined people.

SPIRITUAL KEYSTONE HABITS

If my goal is to become a greater follower of Jesus, then it's important that I have habits that point me to this goal—and not all good habits are created equal. I want to find spiritual keystone habits that will spill over like dominoes into other areas of my life. These keystone habits can then become the system to accomplish my goals. So where would I be able to find the keystone spiritual habits I should shoot for?

In Jesus!

Eugene Peterson paraphrased Jesus' words in Matthew 11:29: **"Walk with me and work with me—watch how I do it. Learn the unforced rhythms of grace."**

Jesus invites us to follow Him. As we walk with Him and work with Him, we look to Him—and He teaches us "the unforced rhythms of grace." That's what I love about the habits of Jesus. I don't acquire them by asserting more of my willpower. They're unforced. They come naturally from an internal desire to follow Jesus and become more like Him.

Most people think that in order to follow Jesus, they just have to power through, grit their teeth, pull up their bootstraps, and just try harder. But tenacious self-effort isn't the abundant life! He gives us His grace, and His grace brings these habits into our lives. Pastor John Ortberg observes, "Habits eat willpower for breakfast."

And as we develop the unforced rhythms of Jesus, we're touched by His heart and changed from the inside out so that we resemble Him more and more. This is the end goal. The goal of our being in relationship with Jesus is that we will become more like Him. Grace empowers us to want to be the best followers of Jesus that we can be.

Paul says it this way to Timothy: **"Discipline yourself for the purpose of godliness." 1 Timothy 4:7**

Keystone habits enable us to become more like Christ.

Over the next 40 days, my challenge for you is to practice the five keystone habits of Jesus so they become a part of your life. They will help you grow in your relationship with God, which will ultimately help you become a greater follower of Jesus Christ. Great followers of Jesus are in a great relationship with God.

Maybe I've convinced you of the importance of the right habits. Many of you will want to jump in, start setting goals, and conquer them, but the wisest thing you can do is start small. There's amazing power in the small choices you make.

I believe this statement: People often overestimate what they can do in the short-term and underestimate what they can do in the long-term.

GREAT FOLLOWERS OF JESUS ARE IN A GREAT RELATIONSHIP WITH GOD.

An ancient Chinese proverb says, "A journey of a thousand miles starts with a single step." All of us are capable of one small step. The end goal may seem way out there, but if we take one step toward the goal, and then another, we'll be getting closer and closer, and eventually we'll reach our destination. But of course, it's important to make sure you're walking in the right direction.

It would be tragic if you were taking steps every day only to find that you were going in the wrong direction. That's the case with many people. We walk with good intentions but hit targets nowhere close to Jesus.

That's why this book is taking dead aim at Jesus Christ.

Success is the product of daily habits, not once-in-a-lifetime transformations.

Jerry Seinfeld is one of the greatest comedians of all time. He lives by the goal: "Don't break the chain." He wants to write one joke every day. It doesn't matter if it's good or bad—just write one joke. And when he has written one joke, his mind is already in gear, and he often writes another one and another one. Just don't break the chain . . . write a joke every day.[8] It's a small habit that works for him.

Small habits performed over a long time make a major difference.

Don't underestimate how our God can start something big through a small habit. Our God loves to take small acts of faithfulness and do something special with them. Five loaves and two fish in God's economy equals food for thousands. Faith as small as a mustard seed can move mountains. Salvation for the world comes through a baby in Bethlehem born in a stable and put in a feeding trough.

This 40-day challenge features devotions with daily challenges centered on the five keystone habits of Jesus. Many of the challenges aren't big at all, but these small habits done over a long period of time will produce incredible impact.

MY STORY

I've spent the last few years acquiring new habits. If people looked at my life a few years ago, they may not have noticed much wrong on the outside, but truthfully, there were a few parts of my life that I didn't like.

I had become overweight. I was staying up later and later and fought waking up in the morning. Even when I was awake, I didn't feel productive during hours that I should have been getting a lot done. I fell asleep on the couch 90% of the time, leaving my wife in bed by herself. Of course, I had excuses and lies every time.

At that point, I decided to start working on a few small habits. I set some goals to be a greater husband, a greater father, and a healthier person. Three years later, I'm in the best shape I've ever been in, I can barely stay up past 9:30 PM because I'm no longer a night owl, I'm far more productive at work, and God has given me far more influence than I could have handled just a few years ago. And every night I fall asleep in my bed with my wife.

The change started when I began working on keystone habits and set some goals. While my new physical habits have helped me immensely, I want nothing more than to be a greater follower of Jesus and challenge people of all ages to be greater followers of Jesus. God has been so good to me, so I can't settle for anything less than giving Him my best. That's why I've been on the journey to help others understand what true growth looks like—and it all starts with your relationship with God.

WHAT WILL YOUR STORY BE?

You might be saying, "Well, even if I wanted to change, I can't. I can't even think about good habits because I'm stuck in a life of bad habits. And there's no way out."

Here's the good news. There *is* a way out. The apostle Paul encourages us: **"No temptation has overtaken you except what is common to mankind. And God is faithful; he will not let you be tempted beyond what you can bear. But when you are tempted, he will also provide a way out so that you can endure it." 1 Corinthians 10:13**

Jesus Christ was your way out of sin and death when He went to the cross, and today, He is your way in to a vibrant, life-changing connection with God. Your habits can change. You're a child of God, and you have the Holy Spirit inside you. Paul once persecuted Christians, but he discovered that sudden change is possible. In a flash of light on the road to Damascus, Paul was transformed from being an enemy of Christ to become His champion. He knows about the power of the Holy Spirit. Look at his words from Romans 8:11: **"And if the Spirit of him who raised Jesus from the dead is living in you, he who raised Christ from the dead will also give life to your mortal bodies because of his Spirit who lives in you."**

Living inside you is the same Spirit that raised Jesus Christ from the dead! Paul also writes in 2 Timothy 1:7: **"For the Spirit God gave us does not make us timid, but gives us power, love and self-discipline."**

The very heart of the gospel, the Good News, is that when Jesus Christ comes into your life by grace through faith, you inherit eternal life, and you're changed right then and there. You are a new creation. This is the greatest opportunity in this world! Death can't defeat the Spirit He put inside you. You're powerful, and you're capable of change because God lives in you!

Now that we know how powerful we are because of God's grace and strength, let's grow in our relationship with God by learning to practice the fve keystone habits of Jesus.

THE 40-DAY BEING CHALLENGE IS ON!

DAY 1

COMMIT TO COMMUNITY

When Jesus picked His disciples, He didn't pick the brightest, most successful or most educated people. They came from different professions and backgrounds.

Peter, Andrew, James and John were fisherman and business owners.

Matthew was a tax collector.

Simon was a rebel against the Roman government. He was called a "zealot."

We don't know what Philip, Bartholomew, Thomas, Thaddaeus or James were, but they were probably involved on one of the three most common occupations in Jesus' time: fishing, carpentry, or farming.

All four Gospels show that one of Jesus' first actions when He started His ministry was choosing His disciples. From the very beginning, He was committed to a community of like-minded people.

If anyone could have been self-sufficient, it's Jesus. Actually, the guys He picked were slow to understand who He was and why He came, but Jesus was committed to His community. Why?

Because . . . You aren't meant to be alone.

You're made to be in community.

But the more you look into Jesus' life, you also find that He didn't just have a group of 12 friends. In 1 Corinthians 15, Paul recounts the resurrection story, and in verse 6 he writes, **"He appeared to more than five hundred of the brothers and sisters at the same time."** At that point, Jesus gathered with a group of more than five hundred people. (And earlier, He had been the host for miraculous meals for thousands!)

Jesus had a smaller group. Luke 10:1 says: **"The Lord appointed seventy-two others and sent them two-by-two ahead of him to every town and place where he is about to go."** This is still a large group, but it was people who got more intentional time with Jesus than the 500.

But some relationships were even deeper. Jesus committed to 12 disciples early in His ministry, and the 12 got much more time with Him than the 72. There are at least a couple of dozen recorded times when Jesus took the 12 aside to explain His sermons or parables. During the Last Supper, He demonstrated to these men how He would suffer and die for the sins of all people.

You may be surprised, but it goes even deeper than that. Jesus had an especially close relationship with three of disciples: Peter, James, and John. In Matthew's Gospel alone, we see Jesus take these three with Him three separate times. They had even more access than the 12. He invited them into the home where He raised Jairus' daughter from death in Matthew 5, they saw Jesus transfigured in radiant white in Matthew 17, and they were asked to accompany Him to pray for strength shortly before His death in Matthew 26.

As I thought about Jesus' relationships with these three men, I wondered if I should have friends like these. What traits or characteristics did Peter, James, and John have? Each of them had positive characteristics, but they weren't the sharpest tools in the shed. In fact, in Acts 4, Peter and John are described as "unschooled, ordinary men." And all three of them were pretty hot-tempered. There was a time where Peter cut the ear off of a guard, and Jesus looked back at him and said, "Really, come on Pete" (my translation), and He put the guy's ear back on. James and John weren't much better. Their nickname was "the Sons of Thunder." In Luke 9 we read that Jesus led the disciples into a Samaritan village where the people didn't welcome Him. James and John said to Jesus, "Lord, do you want us to call down fire from heaven to destroy them?"

Talk about tempers!

And it also appears they were pretty competitive. John describes himself as "the disciple Jesus loved," but none of the other writers described him that way. In the accounts of Peter cutting off the guard's ear, John tells us it's Peter, but the other Gospel writers don't mention his name. In the resurrection story, John and Peter ran to the tomb, and John made sure to explain that he got there first.

You would think that Jesus would have had the smartest, most humble group of people around Him, but that's not the picture we get. It shows me that community isn't always neat—it's imperfect, and at times it's tough and awkward. The people in our community won't always get it right. But these 3—and you could argue the 12, the 72, and the 500—had something in common. They were on the same mission. They followed Jesus.

Your community won't always be fun or easy. You'll have conflict with people you are closest to, sometimes over serious things, sometimes over trivial things, and sometimes you'll fight over who's faster. The question I have for you on Day 1 is this:

Is your community following Jesus?

Are the people close to you pursuing Jesus with all their hearts? If they are, then you probably are. If they aren't, then . . .

Your community matters, and whether you know it or not, you're influenced by them.

Jesus had a 500, a 72, a 12, a 3, but He also had a one—God was at the center.

But you can have God at the center and still not be complete. Think about this. God said to Adam, **"It is not good for man to be alone." Genesis 2:18** At that point, Eve wasn't around, but Adam wasn't really alone because God was with Him. But here we find that even Adam's relationship with God wasn't enough. God wired Adam for human relationships and created a companion for him.

I don't buy the line some people say: "Oh, it's just me and God. He's all I need, and that's how it was meant to be." No, that's not necessarily true. God will be with you and for you when perhaps no one else is, but you were created for relationships— with God certainly, but also with others.

We'll dive much deeper into the importance of community on Days 6-12, but for today, ask yourself this one question: Is my community following Jesus?

DAY 2

STUDY SCRIPTURE

Even though Jesus was fully God, He had a regular habit of studying Scripture. This is the second keystone habit we're exploring. Jesus was constantly surrounded by Scripture at the temple or synagogues. In the only recorded story of Jesus as a growing child, He was at the temple learning from the rabbis. At the end of the story, it says, **"And Jesus grew in wisdom and stature, and in favor with God and man." Luke 2:52**

Jesus continued to grow in wisdom, and if you and I want to grow in wisdom, there is no better way to gain wisdom than through the Scriptures.

In the Gospels alone, I counted about 80 instances of Jesus quoting Old Testament Scripture, so it's clear that Jesus had a thorough understanding of the Bible of His day. Now we have the New Testament as well, and today, the Old and New Testaments combined are referred to as the Scriptures. Pastor and author Tim Keller remarked that there are 1800 Bible verses where Jesus is speaking . . . those red letters in your Bible, and 180 of them are Him quoting Scripture. That's 10%. That's amazing! I wonder what it would be like if 10% of the things out of my mouth were Scripture.

Studying the Scriptures allows us to see our true identity. In fact, let me illustrate this point from the life of Jesus. Just after Jesus was raised from the dead, He had a startling encounter with the disciples. They had heard reports that He was alive, but they were still uncertain. In Luke's account, Jesus suddenly appeared in the room.

"While they were still talking about this, Jesus himself stood among them and said to them, 'Peace be with you.'" Luke 24:36

In the middle of their debate about whether Jesus actually was alive again, Jesus just burst in! This is what our God can do—and what He still does today. Some of you are reading this right now, and you're wondering about the reality of God. Amazingly, He can come to you, right now in this moment. As you open God's Word, He can burst into your heart and change everything for you.

When the other Gospel writers record this event, they add the detail that Jesus came through the wall. He didn't break it down; He just appeared. How's that for an entrance? Luke puts us in the scene:

"They were startled and frightened, thinking they saw a ghost. He said to them, 'Why are you troubled, and why do doubts rise in your minds? Look at my hands and my feet. It is I myself! Touch me and see; a ghost does not have flesh and bones, as you see I have.'" Luke 24:37-39

Jesus then begins to teach them one last thing before He ascends.

"He said to them, 'This is what I told you while I was still with you: Everything must be fulfilled that is written about me in the Law of Moses, the Prophets and the Psalms.'" Luke 24:44

Jesus points to the importance of each part of the Old Testament: The Law of Moses, the Prophets, and the Psalms. Jesus was declaring that all of the prophecies He had taught them had to happen. They had to be fulfilled, and He was the one who fulfilled them.

Then look at what Jesus does:

> **"Then he opened their minds so they could understand the Scriptures."**
> **Luke 24:45**

One of the very last things Jesus does on Earth is open the Scriptures and explain God's truth to the disciples. He's about to leave them and ascend back to heaven, but before He goes, He explains again what's written about Him in the Old Testament.

This is why churches open the Bible on Sunday mornings in worship and offer Bible studies and small groups. There's something powerful about opening the Bible and talking about it together. It contains the greatest story of love ever told, and its words are still active and alive today. They have incredible power. We're changed by them.

> **"He told them, 'This is what is written: The Messiah will suffer and rise**
> **from the dead on the third day, and repentance for the forgiveness of sins**
> **will be preached in his name to all nations, beginning at Jerusalem.'"**
> **Luke 24:46-47**

Jesus didn't want them to miss the big point. Let me paraphrase it: "In case all the hints and clues haven't dawned on you yet, I'm the Messiah. I had to suffer and rise. I'm God in the flesh. I've revealed myself to you. I'm showing you who I am." And finally, this:

> **"You are witnesses of these things. I am going to send you what my Father**
> **has promised; but stay in the city until you have been clothed with power**
> **from on high." Luke 24:48-49**

He's saying, "Now that I've told you who I am, let me tell you who you are. You are witnesses of these things. I'm asking you to go and share your testimony, share your story, share what you saw, the things that happened. And as you go, I'm going to send you my Holy Spirit so that when I leave, you don't go alone. You'll go with My power!"

In Jesus' final moments with the disciples before He ascends, He opens up the Scriptures and teaches them. He did two things that Scripture still does for us, and He did them in this order:

1 He explained who He was.

2 He explained who they were in light of that.

This is the power and purpose of the Bible: Studying Scripture helps you discover who God is and who you are.

Jesus is declaring to them, "This is who I am, and this is who I've called you to be." And then He ascends. His work is done.

Jesus' message seems simple to me, and yet we've made it so dense and complex. We find out more about who we are and why we exist as we discover more about our God.

Days 13–19 will help us go deeper in discovering the importance of studying Scripture.

DAY 3

PRIORITIZE PRAYER

In this book, I'm challenging you to grow in your relationship with God. The success of any relationship starts with communication.

The way we communicate has radically changed from just a decade ago, let alone two millennia ago when Jesus walked on Earth. In many ways, modern communication makes life easier, but in other ways our lives have become much more complicated.

Because I was born in 1983, I'm described as a Xennial, who is someone born at the end of Generation X and the beginning of the Millennial generation. Xennials are described as having an analog childhood and a digital adulthood. In other words, we first experienced life without social media and cell phones, but we were early adopters of new technology.

As a Xennial, I remember the days of the computer game *Oregon Trail*. I was so disappointed when one of my kids in the game got dysentery and the disease wiped out the whole family. I also remember the days when children could play outside in a neighbor's backyard without the threat of the police being called. And in many ways, I liked a lot about those days.

But today, we're able to accomplish far more because of technology. I'm grateful that I get to live in an age when we have a little device in our pockets that has up to seven million times the memory and 100,000 times faster processing than the computer that landed a man on a moon just 50 years ago. We're living in a communication age that's unparalleled. But in this rapidly changing world, the best way to communicate with God remains the same.

Prayer is the way we communicate with God.

As I studied the life of Jesus in the four Gospels, I found nearly 50 times that Jesus either practiced prayer or taught on the importance of prayer. Jesus is shown praying alone, praying in public, praying early in the morning, praying in the evening, praying before meals, praying before important decisions, and praying before and after healings. In fact, in one place where Jesus was praying, the disciples were so impressed that they asked Him, "Teach us how to pray." The disciples had certainly prayed before, but there was something about the way Jesus communicated with God that was different. They were saying, "I want to pray like that. Teach me." And that's where we get the words of the Lord's Prayer.

I'm encouraged by the disciples' request. Like them, I've prayed many times, but I must admit that prayer is an area where I want to grow more. I want it, but sometimes it's hard, and I don't know what to do, what to say, or how to grow in my prayer life. It's nice to know I'm not the only one who struggles with this. All of us can grow in this area. So, if prayer isn't one of your strengths, that's okay. You can learn. You can grow.

I want to show you a sampling of how Jesus prioritized prayer.

"Very early in the morning, while it was still dark, Jesus got up, left the house and went off to a solitary place, where he prayed." Mark 1:35

"But Jesus often withdrew to lonely places and prayed." Luke 5:16

"One of those days Jesus went out to a mountainside to pray, and spent the night praying to God." Luke 6:12

These verses are just a small sampling of the times we see Jesus praying. You get the sense that everywhere He went, He was communicating with God the Father and the Holy Spirit. Prayer was a priority in Jesus' life at all times and in all circumstances.

Is prayer a priority in your life?

Let me ask you a question. Look back at the last week of your life: if God answered every one of your prayer requests, what would be different in the world today?

Sadly, if I answered that question for myself, there would be some weeks when the world wouldn't look all that different. My typical prayers, if they were answered, would mean my sermon would be creative and powerful, new people would come to church, the Cleveland Browns would have won their game, my kids would have done well

IF GOD ANSWERED EVERY ONE OF YOUR PRAYER REQUESTS, WHAT WOULD BE **DIFFERENT** IN THE WORLD TODAY?

at school, my wife would have had a great week, a couple of people would have gotten new jobs, and a few healings would have happened, but nothing crazy in the world would have happened most weeks if all my prayers had been answered. That's sad.

Many of us say we believe in the power of prayer, but our prayers show otherwise.

Actually, with all of the technological advancement we've seen, it's become easier to trust in our own power. I've certainly seen this in my life. But if we really believe in the power of God, we'll prioritize prayer.

In Days 20–26, we'll learn more about how to prioritize prayer and begin to use prayer as a first response, not a last resort.

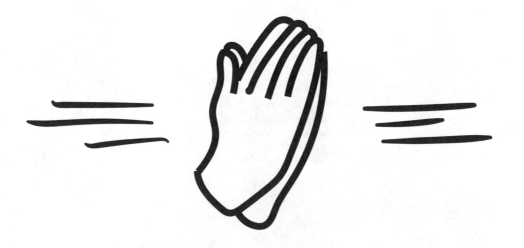

DAY 4

SEEK SOLITUDE

As I read the Gospels and looked for the five keystone habits, I was most surprised at how often Jesus practiced solitude. He had a beautiful balance between being around people and being alone with God.

Sometimes I hear people say that they don't feel connected to God anymore. I tell them, "God wasn't the one who moved away!" In fact, from the beginning of time, God has proven that He longs for a relationship with us. Human beings are the pinnacle of His creation. After He created people, God rested. He didn't rest after He made the stars, the moon, the seas, the earth, the sky, and the animals. He rested after He made human beings. It wasn't that He was tired; He had finished His work, and He wanted to spend time with people. Think about this. The very first time Adam opened his eyes after sleeping a night on Earth, when he woke up on his first full day of living, God was ready to enjoy being with him.

This is the nature of our God. He has made it possible to be in relationship with us. When we, His creation, turned our backs on Him, He sent His Son in human form to relentlessly pursue us and bring us back.

We can get so busy, so preoccupied, that we don't take time to be quiet and connect with God.

<u>The habit of seeking solitude gives us opportunities to simply be in relationship with God.</u>

I often think my life is really busy, but if anyone was busy, it's Jesus. You don't have to read very much in Jesus' story to see just how much He did. I feel a little exhausted just reading the first chapter of Mark's Gospel! Let me show you.

Jesus begins His ministry, and right away He starts preaching the gospel (verses 14-15). Then He calls His disciples (verses 16-20), and they start following Him. He immediately goes into the synagogue and begins to teach. He taught so powerfully that the people were amazed. As He's teaching, a man starts yelling at Jesus—and it's not the good kind of yelling! It's actually a man who is possessed by a demon. Jesus delivers the demon from the man, and from there, He and the disciples go to the home of Peter's mother-in-law. You would think this would be the time Jesus would kick back and rest, but instead, Peter thought, "Well, Jesus is here, and my mother-in-law is sick. I'll get some brownie points with the wife if He'll heal her." So Jesus healed her. It has been a long day. As the sun set, Mark tells us, **"That evening after sunset the people brought to Jesus all the sick and demon-possessed. The whole town gathered at the door, and Jesus healed many who had various diseases. He also drove out many demons." Mark 1:32-34a**

Wow . . . that's quite a day! Aren't you exhausted just thinking about it? Many of us claim we're busy, and we may be, but after reading about a day in the life of Jesus, it's obvious that He wins the busyness award. If I had a day like that, I'd plan on sleeping in the next day, but take a look at what Jesus does:

> **"Very early in the morning, while it was still dark, Jesus got up, left the house and went off to a solitary place, where he prayed." Mark 1:35**

What did Jesus do after an action-packed day? He got alone with God. He knew that to do His work, He needed to be in touch with God. He prayed. He talked with God. We talked about prayer yesterday, but I'm not being redundant. The keystone habits are connected. They work together to enhance each other, and that makes them even more powerful.

This chapter of Mark is only one instance when we see Jesus seeking solitude. When I read through the Gospels of Matthew, Mark, Luke, and John, I found 39 times Jesus practiced or taught on the importance of solitude. Jesus found time to be alone before making decisions and when He began important parts of His work, and He carved out time alone to recharge after the work was completed.

Let me be more specific: Jesus spent 40 days in the wilderness before He began His three-year ministry that would lead Him to the cross. During His ministry, He spent time in solitude before making the important decision to choose His 12 disciples, He spent time in solitude grieving His friend John the Baptist after he was martyred for his faith, and He spent time alone with God before enduring the cross.

If Jesus, who had much more on His plate than I'll ever have on mine, regularly and often sought alone time with God, how much more important is it for me to find time alone with Him?

We live in a loud and distracting world that consumes our attention and pulls us in many different directions. To truly discover and fulfill God's purpose for us, we must spend regular time with God.

In Days 27–33, we'll be seeking solitude and find the focus that we need to be the people God calls us to be.

TO TRULY DISCOVER AND FULFILL GOD'S PURPOSE FOR US, WE MUST SPEND REGULAR TIME WITH GOD.

DAY 5

CHOOSE CHURCH

I remember a particular summer day in Florida. I know it's hard to believe, but it was really hot and really humid. My family and I were looking forward to going to the neighborhood pool for a swim to cool off. When we got there, we were told that we couldn't get in the pool. The man explained that it would be dangerous to swim because they had just "shocked" the pool. He told us it happens once a week. Why they chose in the middle of the day was beyond me, but whatever the reason, we had to wait.

This is a common practice. They use chlorine to kill contaminants, including germs from bodily fluids like sweat and urine, which gets in the water . . . but not from anyone I know, of course. In a sermon one Sunday, I asked people to raise their hands if they had peed in a pool, and only one person was brave enough to be truthful—even though two-thirds of Americans do it. Whatever the statistics may be, pools must be shocked with chlorine to kill the germs so it's safe to swim.

Believe it or not, this is a beautiful image of living on mission and doing what Jesus calls us to do. When we interact with people in our neighborhoods, parks, jobs, restaurants, and everywhere else, we're exposed to "germs" of brokenness and darkness. We're bombarded by bad news, and we actually welcome it because it fascinates us. The more we get out into the world and connect with people who need Jesus, the more we're exposed to the world's contaminants.

Quite often, my body, my brain, and my soul need a shock. I need a place where it can go to consistently hear good news . . . to shock my system back.

The church, the gathering of God's people, is the place I go to get my system shocked. I know that churches look different from one another, but when the church is done right and the assembly is gathered, it's the place where we regularly hear the proclamation of the unparalleled, and dare I say "shocking," Good News of Jesus Christ.

Of the five keystone habits of Jesus, this is the one that wasn't on my initial list. But after analyzing the accounts of Jesus' ministry, it was clear that this one needed to be included.

There are several places in the Bible that tell us that Jesus chose church. Jesus loved being in the temple in Jerusalem and in synagogues throughout the country. A synagogue simply means an "assembly" or "congregation," so it was very similar to our church services. When Jesus was a boy, He was in the temple talking with the elders, and when He was older, He was often in places of worship. In the week before the crucifixion, Jesus was in Jerusalem, and Luke tells us, **"Each day Jesus was teaching at the temple." Luke 21:37**

Jesus not only went to the temple and the synagogues to teach, but also for praise, prayer, and worship. Many of the church practices we have today are based on the worship of the Jewish people in their synagogues. For instance, they read from the Scriptures just like we do; they sang the psalms, just like we sing hymns and other songs; they devoted time to worship, and we have regular times to meet together; and they donated money for the ministry just like we do.

The church today shares some similarities to the temple and synagogues in Jesus' day, but in many ways, it looks and feels different. Still, worshipping with God's people is something Jesus practiced and modeled for His disciples.

Sadly, more and more people are walking away from the church today, but it has happened before. That's why the author of Hebrews said, **"Don't give up on meeting together, as some are already doing." Hebrews 10:25.** It's important for the church to be God's representatives in the world, to truly be His hands and feet. To be passionate and knowledgeable about God, we need to worship together regularly.

I've been pondering this question a lot lately: Can you truly love Jesus without choosing church?

Think about it. Jesus instituted the church. At the end of time, when Jesus comes back, the Bible says that He'll return for "His bride," which is the church. The church wasn't optional to Jesus. It has been, is, and always will be central to His plan. Can you really love Jesus without choosing church?

Choosing church brings consistency into our lives. It reminds us of God's infinite love, grace, and power. The church is the consistent place where the Good News of Jesus is proclaimed.

Take a look at the beginning of Jesus' ministry. It's in Luke, chapter 4.

> **"He went to Nazareth, where he had been brought up, and on the Sabbath day he went into the synagogue, as was his custom. He stood up to read, and the scroll of the prophet Isaiah was handed to him. Unrolling it, he found**

the place where it is written: 'The Spirit of the Lord is on me, because he has anointed me to proclaim good news to the poor. He has sent me to proclaim freedom for the prisoners and recovery of sight for the blind, to set the oppressed free, to proclaim the year of the Lord's favor.'" Luke 4:16-19

I can picture this moment. They didn't have phones to scroll through to find a particular verse, and they didn't have books. They handed Jesus a scroll. The practice was to read sequentially, so when the scroll was handed to Jesus, He simply unrolled it to reveal the reading for the day, which just happened to be the 61st chapter of Isaiah. It wasn't a coincidence that this was the passage for the day. It announced the coming of the Messiah. Jesus was reading about Himself!

"Then he rolled up the scroll, gave it back to the attendant and sat down. The eyes of everyone in the synagogue were fastened on him. He began by saying to them, 'Today this scripture is fulfilled in your hearing.'" Luke 4:20-21

This was the modern-day mic drop. #ScrollDrop

Jesus was declaring right there in the assembly that He is the Good News!

This is why church is so important. It gives us an opportunity to open the Word of God and declare the reason Jesus came: to announce Good News to the poor, freedom to the prisoner, sight to the blind, release for the oppressed, and to proclaim the year of the Lord's favor. When we gather as the assembly, we get to tell one another the shocking Good News of Jesus Christ.

In Days 34–40, we'll dive deeper as to why and how we can choose church today.

KEYSTONE HABIT 1:

COMM
COMM

IT TO
UNITY

DAY 6

WIRED FOR RELATIONSHIPS

One of the most confusing concepts in the Christian faith is the Trinity, which asserts that God is Father, Son, and Holy Spirit, and has existed this way for all of eternity. And yet, these three persons form one God. Even from the beginning, God the Father, God the Son, and God the Holy Spirit existed together as a community of love. C. S. Lewis, the great theologian, describes the Trinity this way:

> "[God is] a dynamic, pulsating activity, a life, almost a kind of drama. Almost, if you will not think me irreverent, a kind of dance. The union between the Father and the Son is such a live concrete thing that this union itself is also a person. It is as if a sort of communal personality came into existence."[9]

We were created in God's image (Genesis 1:26), so from the beginning, we've been created for community.

God declared that His creation of Adam was "very good," but in the first words God ever spoke to mankind, He said: **"It is not good for the man to be alone."** **Genesis 2:18.** After this, God gave Eve to Adam.

Sadly, many people experience loneliness today.

A 2018 study by Global Health Service company CIGNA found that 46% of U.S. adults feel lonely sometimes or always. 47% report feeling left out.[10] That's almost half of our country, and the numbers are rising among the younger generation. In a decade, the number will be the majority. People have settled for fake, inauthentic, cyber relationships, and it's taking a toll on us.

Some of the most popular television programs in recent years are *The Office*, *Seinfeld*, and *This Is Us*. Why do we get drawn into these shows? It's more than the comedy and the drama. It's the fact that these shows depict close relationships that many of us yearn for. Why? Because God made us to yearn for them.

Our brains are wired to be in community so we can be authentic.

Psychologist Judith E. Glaser is the author of *Conversational Intelligence*. She explains:

> *"There is a part of our brain that has a massive impact on us— and one that explains deep connection. This part of the brain is called the Temporoparietal Junction, or the TPJ. This part of our brain is activated when we share with others. When we actively share with others: sharing deep secrets, sharing what's on our mind, sharing our fears, our dreams and our aspirations, the brain lights up like a Christmas tree. This is why people get addicted to tweeting and texting—we are sharing transparently without judging or filtering. This behavior activates a high level of oxytocin, which is the neurotransmitter that enables us to bond and connect with others deeply."[11]*

Dr. Glaser is saying that it feels really, really good to share life with others. In fact, talking with others about things that matter is imperative for our emotional well-being.

Relationships are like a dance. Sometimes we can dance well. We can move in rhythm with our dance partner, but other times, we can step on each other's toes or dance to our own beat.

But as hard as community may be, I've found that people who are connected in Christian community tend to walk closely with Christ throughout their lives, but those who are isolated tend to make bigger mistakes and are far more likely to give up on their faith.

In my study, I've seen that many of the heroes in the Bible had a close and trusted friend. Rarely—that is, almost never—does God call a person to go it alone. Moses had Aaron. David had Jonathan. Elijah had Elisha. Paul had Barnabas and Silas. When Jesus sent the disciples out, He sent them in pairs. Even the animals that got on Noah's ark came in two-by-two!

Who is in your community? On Day 1 we looked at the different groups in Jesus' life. I want us revisit the way Jesus formed His community and see how we can pattern our relationships after His. Jesus had 3, 12, 72, and 500. Who are your 3, 12, 72, and 500? Don't get hung up on the exact numbers. We're looking at the principles underneath these numbers.

Who are your 3? These are the people you allow the greatest access into your life through time and influence. They're your spouse and perhaps some family members or your best friends.

Who are your 12? These people spend a lot of time with you and are very influential. They could be family members, close friends, maybe even a few people in your small group or at your church.

OUR BRAINS ARE WIRED TO BE IN COMMUNITY SO WE CAN BE AUTHENTIC.

Who are your 72? As the circle widens, you may think of groups of people, not just individuals. It could be the parents you see at your son's baseball games or the ones you interact with at your daughter's dance club. It could be your neighbors, your small group, and your extended family that you see once or twice a year.

And finally, who are your 500? These people are larger groups, such as classmates where you went to school, those in other departments at your work, and people who are "friends" on social networks. This group might include some whose name you don't even know (or that you can't remember), but you see them from time to time.

As you connect with others in each of these expanding spheres of relationships, I'm praying for you what Jesus prayed in John 17 as He prayed for our unity:

> **"With I in them and you in me, I pray that they may become perfectly one, so that the world may know that you sent me and loved them even v you loved me." John 17:23**

When we reflect the love of God in our unity with one another, the world sees who Jesus is.

CHALLENGE

WHO IS YOUR COMMUNITY?

Who are the people in your expanding rings of relationships? Fill in the spheres to identify your 3, 12, 72, and 500 and ask yourself: "Does my community encourage me to be closer to Jesus?"

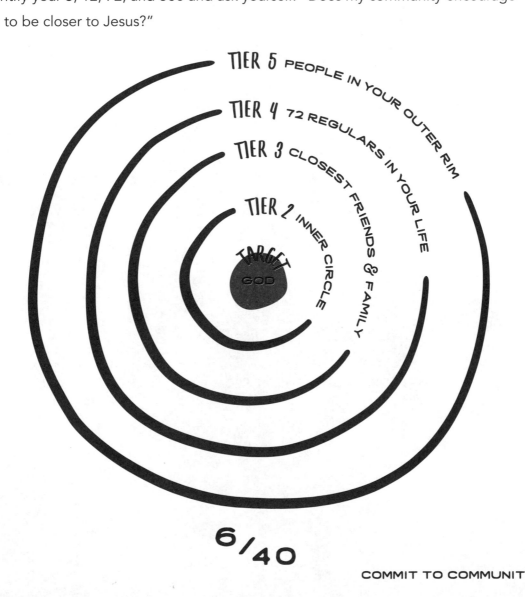

TIER 5 PEOPLE IN YOUR OUTER RIM

TIER 4 72 REGULARS IN YOUR LIFE

TIER 3 CLOSEST FRIENDS & FAMILY

TIER 2 INNER CIRCLE

TARGET GOD

6/40

DAY 7

THE POWER OF CHRISTIAN COMMUNITY

In the early part of 2014, I felt a stirring in my heart to teach the Bible on a deeper level. Many people were starting to attend our church, and I realized most of them didn't have a biblical worldview. How could I teach them the entire Bible in one setting but make it entertaining and fun? After a lot of prayer and deliberation, I decided to attempt to break a Guinness World Record for the Longest Speech Marathon. I set a target date of November 7-9 and started planning.

The more I dug into the rules and the red tape behind a Guinness World Record attempt, I realized I was in way over my head. Though the record has an individual's name attached to it, I discovered that it required a team effort. We quickly put together teams of people to help, from logistics to technical aspects to advertising. We even had a team to ensure we were meeting all the rules and regulations from Guinness.

We also decided to use this event for a fundraiser to support Hand in Hand, a new non-profit that helps men recovering from addiction. We would use the funds from the event to help them purchase their first recovery home.

As the weekend approached, I was incredibly nervous. It was, in fact, a marathon of speaking. As it went on and on and on, God showed up in the lives of many people. We broke the world record as I preached through the Bible for 53 hours.

and 18 minutes (And you thought your pastor's sermons were long!), and we raised more than $100,000 for Hand in Hand.

While the record has my name attached to it, it took well over 200 people to play their parts. It reminded me of the importance of community. I may be able to do something great, but a community of people can help me do something even greater.

Does your community inspire you to greater things?

There is power in community, positively or negatively. One of the reasons I wanted to get in better physical shape isn't only because I knew I needed to, but also because I had just seen a friend transform himself. His example inspired me. I asked him to tell me how he did it. I did some of the same exercises and lifts that he did and even bought the protein powders he used. His tenacity and commitment helped me in an important area of my life.

This isn't just a principle that applies to our bodies. It can help spiritually as well. Let me explain.

Arguably, one of the most beautiful trees in North America is the aspen. It's an amazing tree. Actually, each tree isn't a single organism. A group of aspen trees, known as a "clone," is considered a single organism. Underground, the root systems of acres and acres of aspen trees are connected. When you look at a forest of aspen trees, you're looking at a single organism, and each part supports the others by sharing nutrients.

The taller trees catch the sun and send nutrients down to the smaller trees that aren't in the sunlight, and the smaller trees are pulling the nutrients up from the soil and sending them to the taller trees. It's this beautiful picture of each tree contributing to the health and success of all the others. To look at it the other way, each tree needs the help from the entire community in order to stand out in its beauty and strength.

The aspen forest is a wonderful picture of Christian community. God has given each of us gifts and talents and has called us to share what He has given so all of us can represent Him more effectively.

Paul says it this way in Romans 12:4-5: **"For just as each of us has one body with many members, and these members do not all have the same function, so in Christ we, though many, form one body, and each member belongs to all the others."**

To be the greatest representative of Jesus, we need each person to do his or her part. It's important to remember that while God has given each of us a gift, He hasn't given any of us every gift. One of our biggest problems comes when we elevate ourselves in pride or lower ourselves in discouragement. All of us play a part—it's only a part, but it's an important part.

When we bring our gifts together to help one another, amazing things are possible.

During our week of Choose Church, we'll dive deeper into helping you discover your spiritual gifts.

CHALLENGE

WHO CAN HELP?

Identify one person in each of the five habits of Jesus who excels in that particular habit. Reach out to one of them and ask that person to share goals, habits, challenges, and benefits of the habit.

FIVE KEYSTONE HABITS	1. COMMIT TO COMMUNITY
2. STUDY SCRIPTURE	3. PRIORITIZE PRAYER
4. SEEK SOLITUDE	5. CHOOSE CHURCH

Who did you reach out to?

_____

What consistent choices have helped them excel?

_____

_____

_____

7/40

DAY 8

COMMUNITY INFLUENCES YOU

The first keystone habit of Jesus was that He was committed to community. This habit is especially important because there is probably no more important predictor of your future than to look at your present community.

You may not always feel it, but your community has a profound impact on you, for better or worse.

A few decades ago, people rarely moved from one town to another, but today, transportation and mobility have given people the opportunity to relocate. The average person in America moves 11.4 times in a lifetime.[12] "Community" is derived from the word *communite* which means "joint ownership." This implies a physical togetherness and historically referred to geographical location.[13]

But more recently, the word community has been redefined— it's less about being from somewhere and more about being like someone. Studies have shown that we become like who we hang out with.

The closer you are to someone, you're more likely to have the same habits. A study tracked 12,000 people over a 32-year period to determine the impact of close relationships. The researchers found that if you have one friend who is significantly overweight, you are 57% more likely to be overweight. And that's with only one friend.[14] So, it's not the bacon cheeseburgers you eat for breakfast; your love handles are your friend's fault! The reason you don't have great abs is because of your friends, it's not you!

On the other hand, the study found that if one person loses a significant amount of weight, one of three close friends will also lose a significant amount.

The people we hang with significantly shape our habits and our bodies, but it doesn't take a modern study to prove this point. Long before there were any studies like these, Solomon wrote, **"If you walk with the wise, you become wise but a companion of fools suffers harm." Proverbs 13:20**

Schwab's 2019 Modern Wealth Survey just came out and this was one of their conclusions:

> *"3 in 5 Americans pay more attention to how their friends spend their money compared to how they save their own money. An equal number say they're at a loss to understand how their friends are able to afford the expensive vacations and trendy restaurant meals they portray on social media ... Financial decisions are influenced by friends' showy social media feeds. The burden to keep up with the Joneses has been part of our culture for decades, but it appears that social media and the fear of missing out (FOMO) have increased the pressure to spend."[15]*

Another study by Harvard Professor David McClelland tracked people and their communities over a 30-year period and discovered that 95% of our success or failure in life is determined by the people we habitually associate with.[16] As we look to form habits, it's hard, nearly impossible, to make much progress with the other habits if we're not in a supportive community. That's why this one comes before all the others.

When we commit to community, we find that even if we all come from different walks of life, we still have a profound impact on each other. We have different jobs, talents and gifts, and we see things from different angles, but as we meet together, our varied talents and treasures intermix, just like copper and tin. Combining ideas is often the beginning of a brand-new and better idea, like bronze. That's Jesus' plan for community.

If we become like the people in our closest community, and if we want to be more like Jesus, we need to consider whether our community is leading us to be more Christlike . . . or less.

Mark shows us a beautiful picture of community done right:

> "A few days later, when Jesus again entered Capernaum, the people heard that he had come home. They gathered in such large numbers that there was no room left, not even outside the door, and he preached the word to them. Some men came, bringing to him a paralyzed man, carried by four of them. Since they could not get him to Jesus because of the crowd, they made an opening in the roof above Jesus by digging through it and then lowered the mat the man was lying on. When Jesus saw their faith, he said to the paralyzed man, 'Son, your sins are forgiven.'
> Now some teachers of the law were sitting there, thinking to themselves, 'Why does this fellow talk like that? He's blaspheming! Who can forgive sins but God alone?'

THERE IS PROBABLY NO MORE IMPORTANT PREDICTOR OF YOUR FUTURE THAN TO LOOK AT YOUR PRESENT COMMUNITY.

Immediately Jesus knew in his spirit that this was what they were thinking in their hearts, and he said to them, 'Why are you thinking these things? Which is easier: to say to this paralyzed man, "Your sins are forgiven," or to say, "Get up, take your mat and walk"? But I want you to know that the Son of Man has authority on earth to forgive sins.' So he said to the man, 'I tell you, get up, take your mat and go home.' He got up, took his mat and walked out in full view of them all. This amazed everyone and they praised God, saying, 'We have never seen anything like this!'"
Mark 2:1-12

What a powerful example of four friends who literally carried their friend-in-need to Jesus. Without these friends, the paralyzed man never could have gotten to Jesus. Today, a lot of people debate if and how God heals, but in this case, we can see that Jesus forgave and healed the man after looking at the faith of his four friends! If Jesus looked at your friends, would He be amazed at their faith?

CHALLENGE

THE FUTURE YOU

Imagine your life ten years from now. List five things you would like to be true about "the future you." Look at your groups of "3 and 12" from Day 6. Carefully analyze how each group is affecting you in these keystone habits:

1 _____

2 _____

3 _____

4 _____

5 _____

As you reflect on this, who in your groups of 3 and 12 that you identified from Day 6's challenge could push you to be the "future you" that you want to become?

_____

_____

_____

_____

8/40

DAY 9

COMMUNITY HELPS YOU FIND PURPOSE

God has wired us for relationships and for purpose. When we're living the way God intended, community and purpose flow together beautifully.

Alarming new studies show that in the United States, 70% of people are unhappy in their careers and aren't motivated by what they do,[17] and 98% of people die without fulfilling their dreams.[18]

For most people, their biggest regret isn't sadness or shame over something they've done; their chief regret is about something they didn't do.[19] Too many people are living purposeless lives.

This question of purpose has been around since the beginning of time. In his book, *The Call*, Os Guinness explains that there are multiple answers to our question about purpose, but each answer depends first and foremost on what you believe, and for Christians, who we believe in. Guinness says the biblical answer is that "an infinite personal God has created us in his image and calls us into relationship with himself. Our life-purpose therefore comes from two sources at once—who we are created to be and who we are called to be."[20]

It all starts with two words from Jesus that changed the lives of the disciples, and they change our lives as well: "Follow Me."

Many people are waiting on God to speak from heaven and tell them what they should do with their lives, but in reality, God has already spoken. We have the Bible, and if you read it, you'll find that God has already given us many different ways to live out our purpose. In fact, let me show you four clear things you could do right now:

"Defend the weak and the fatherless; uphold the cause of the poor and the oppressed." Psalm 82:3

"He has shown you, O mortal, what is good. And what does the Lord require of you? To act justly and to love mercy and to walk humbly with your God." Micah 6:8

"And he said to them, 'Go into all the world and proclaim the gospel to the whole creation.'" Mark 16:15

"Religion that God our Father accepts as pure and faultless is this: to look after orphans and widows in their distress and to keep oneself from being polluted by the world." James 1:27

As you read the Bible, you'll find that God has given us many different ways to live out our faith in Him. Stop waiting for God to speak audibly and realize He's already spoken. Start fulfilling one of these purposes today.

Winston Churchill said, "What is the use of living, if it be not to strive for noble causes and to make this muddled world a better place for those who will live in it after we are gone?"[21] I wholeheartedly agree.

But how do we know what "one thing" God has for us?

If you're struggling with purpose or community, here's what I recommend: Find people who are living for a noble cause and join them. This is how community and purpose come together in a beautiful way.

We're all different, and different needs and causes pull on our heartstrings. What is it that pulls on your heartstrings? Is there anyone you know that's living for a noble cause you can join?

God isn't random. He has placed certain gifts and desires in you for a reason, and He has also placed certain people in your life for a reason.

The community that you're already in could be—and probably is—the place where your purpose is realized.

For me, there is no cause more noble than the cause of Jesus Christ and His local church. We'll talk more on Days 34–40 about the importance of church today, but if you've had a hard time finding a clear, compelling sense of purpose, why not join your talents and passions with people in a local church and together bring Christ to the world?

When you join with others and do something meaningful together, you experience the community God has you for, and you experience great fulfillment as you live out your purpose.

In the past two years, on the days right after Christmas, my family has gone on a mission trip with my church. It's been a good rhythm for us to serve people who

FIND PEOPLE WHO ARE LIVING FOR A NOBLE CAUSE AND JOIN THEM.

are disadvantaged, especially after a months-long push toward consumerism in our culture. It's a nice way to flush out the system and remember why we're here.

On the first of these trips, we replaced some roofs on the homes of those who had been impacted by Hurricane Irma in 2017. I honestly wasn't sure how my family would do. Personally, I'm terrible at construction, and I don't enjoy working with my hands. My kids were only 7 and 11, and at home we have a hard time getting them to pick up their clothes or help with the dishes. How were they going to handle construction? The only one I wasn't worried about was my wife. But what I saw during those days was incredible. My kids loved serving people. The place we stayed made a Holiday Inn look like the Ritz-Carlton. The showers were cold and the amenities were nonexistent, but there was something about being together and serving people that gave us incredible joy. Actually, going back home was pretty emotional because my kids wanted to stay and serve. They started chanting in unison, "We want to help the poor!" It was an incredibly moving experience for our family.

Sometimes God calls you to serve alone. That can be enriching, but it's even more fulfilling when you live out your purpose with others. In those moments we experience great fulfillment.

Who do you know who's living for a noble cause? How can you join them?

CHALLENGE

WHAT REALLY PULLS ON YOUR HEARTSTRINGS?

If you had to live for a cause, what cause would you live for?

_____

_____

Identify three people in your world who are living for a noble cause.

1 _____

2 _____

3 _____

What are specific ways you can join them?

_____

_____

_____

_____

As a bonus, it would be an amazing blessing to encourage those three people listed above in a some way, shape, or form.

9/40

DAY 10

COMMUNITY IN A DIGTIAL WORLD

When FaceTime was introduced a few years ago, a series of commercials highlighted this amazing advance in technology. Not only could you talk with someone across the world, but you could see the person. For some reason, I distinctly remember a particular commercial that featured a dad who was a businessman. He flew across the country, checked into his hotel room, and then FaceTimed home so that he could sing Happy Birthday to his seven-year old son. The message was clear and strong: It's very cool to be able to connect face-to-face, even if it's virtual.

But for some strange reason, the commercial left me feeling empty. Yes, it's cool that the dad can be a part of his son's birthday celebration, but I realized that it's not as good as if the dad were actually home and singing with his son. We live in a world that wants to convince us that virtual relationships are as good as real, face-to-face relationships. They're not. If my son hits a home run at his T-Ball game, it's good to see him step on home plate on a video screen, but it's even better to be in the stands, cheering wildly and embracing him as he runs past the stands to the dugout.

I want to be clear. I believe that all of the technological and communication advancements are wonderful, and apps like FaceTime that help us communicate with others are incredible, but they're not the primary place where community takes place. When cyber-relationships become your primary connections, it can lead to devastating consequences.

Our society has seen a significant rise in anxiety and depression since 2011, and especially among teenagers. As Cal Newport points out in his excellent book, *Digital Minimalism*, the number of teenagers owning their own smartphone dramatically increased in that year.[22]

Jean Twenge, San Diego State psychology professor, observed, "The use of social media and smartphones look culpable for the increase in teen mental-health issues." In her article for the *Atlantic* entitled "Have Smartphones Destroyed a Generation?", she added, "It's enough for an arrest—and as we get more data, it might be enough for a conviction."[23]

It's becoming obvious even among our younger generations that connecting in person is becoming socially awkward. That's why in 2017, in a *USA Today* article, Millennials claimed that going on a date is more intimate than having sex.[24] Friendships online don't require as much vulnerability, so most people settle for that. You can keep others at a distance, connect on your own time, at the level you choose, and bail out whenever you want to.

Many parents are having difficulty figuring out how to parent their children's use of digital devices and screen time. While it's easy to blame teenagers and Millennials, many adults are struggling just as much with their own screen usage.

Far too many of us have traded real in-person relationship for cyber-relationships. We can do better...we have to do better. The technology isn't the real problem. We can use all the advances to build better relationships instead of replacing those relationships.

We're living in a different time and a different setting, but the problem isn't new. The author of Hebrews pleaded with Christians to have real, meaningful connections. Look at his words:

" . . . not giving up meeting together, as some are in the habit of doing, but encouraging one another—and all the more as you see the Day approaching." Hebrews 10:25

Something special happens when we meet together. The New Testament contains over 100 instances of the phrase "one another"—which is the translation of the Greek word, *allelon*. We can't experience "one another" alone! We have to be in real relationships with other believers to encourage, support, love, forgive, and accept one another.

I believe in the power of small groups. Even in a digital age, I hear countless stories in my church of lives being changed through small groups. But I also hear people say they can't join one because it takes too much time. I'll be the first to admit that I can get very busy and adding one more activity seems like too much. But when I look at how much time I spend checking out websites and watching online videos, I realize I just might have more time than I thought. The hours are there...and I can decide how to use them. As we look at the life of Jesus, an incredibly busy man, we find more than two dozen times that He pulled the disciples away from their routine to spend time with them. I'm sure there were many more, but these are the ones mentioned in the Gospels. The practice of getting away with a smaller group of people is as important today as it was then. It's easy to get caught up in the demands and pulled in all kinds of directions. If we don't take time to get insights from other believers and give and receive love, we won't be able to live the way God wants us to live. Time with one another isn't optional.

CHALLENGE

SCREEN TIME CHECK

Phone apps give you the ability to assess your screen time. How much time each day did you spend in the last week on your screens? What's your average daily usage?

_____ : _____   _____ : _____

WEEKLY SCREEN TIME   **DAILY SCREEN TIME**

As you examine your screen time, what are the top five apps you used, and how much time do you spend using each of them?

1 _____   ____ : ____

2 _____   ____ : ____

3 _____   ____ : ____

4 _____   ____ : ____

5 _____   ____ : ____

After assessing your screen time, what's one change you could make that would move you toward more authentic relationships?

_____

_____

10/40

DAY 11

THE SNEAKY ENEMY OF INDIVIDUALISM

Yesterday we talked about how our digital world can make us more isolated when it's our primary source of relationships. But there's another factor that builds walls between people. In fact, it's so ingrained in us that we don't even notice it: individualism. We're not on guard against it. We usually celebrate it.

Individualism is the habit of being independent and self-reliant. Many in our country are fiercely proud of their individualism, and as a result, they rely on their own strength, intellect, and talent rather than working with others. The rest of us aren't immune. We believe that we're more productive and deserve more credit if we accomplish something on our own. In the business world, some leaders don't want to train someone else because, they claim, "It's easier if I do it myself." There may be several different excuses for leaders insisting on doing things alone, but it limits delegation and training, and therefore, it keeps others from developing while it adds more burdens to the leader's workload.

Self-reliance is woven into the American Dream, which tells us that anyone, no matter what circumstances they were born into, can attain success through hard work and sacrifice. The ultimate goal is often status, fame, power, and piles of money and possessions. If we have these, the promise says, we'll be happy and fulfilled. But will we?

This concept has a major flaw. Many of the those who have fulfilled the American Dream and risen to the pinnacle of success are miserable. Having more power, prestige, and possessions can't fill the gaping hole in their hearts . . . or ours. If we pursue them as the ultimate aim in life, we'll end up empty, discouraged, and angry that life hasn't worked out the way we expected.

In order to achieve happiness, many people sacrifice the things that bring meaning. They work too hard, putting career above people. They worry too much, always comparing their success with others. And they use people as stepping stones to reach their goals instead of loving them. Sadly, close friends and family, and even their relationship with God, take a back seat to career advancement. They devote countless hours to climb the corporate ladder, and they find excuses to skip church on Sunday and small group involvement during the week. They're just too busy.

For many people, the American Dream has become an American nightmare. When they achieved it, they've found that it's empty. I can think of very few things more depressing than to give your life to a purpose, achieve it, and then realize it was worthless.

An author who challenges me is David Platt. In his book *Radical*, he "implores you to consider the urgent need before us to forsake the American dream now in favor of radical abandonment to the person and purpose of Christ."[25]

When Jesus says, "Follow Me," He's asking us to trust His wisdom, His strength, and His direction instead of being self-reliant. Jesus is inviting us to give up our self-reliance and come into a relationship with Him.

The American Dream is the opposite of the gospel of grace. The Good News of Jesus starts by examining ourselves and finding that we fall short of what God has asked of us. The deeper we look into ourselves, the more we realize we're tragically flawed. Even our best efforts fall far short. We can't remedy the problem by trying harder, relying on our ability to make life work, and impressing God with our performance. No, we realize we can't make it on our own. We need forgiveness. We need a Savior. And all day every day as believers, we need to rely on God's love, forgiveness, and power. Apart from Him, we're weak.

We find the words God gave the apostle Paul to be true of us as well: **"My grace is sufficient for you, for my power is made perfect in weakness . . . for when I am weak, then I am strong."**[26]

Paul is reminding us that we're not saved by our performance and goodness, but through the life, death, and resurrection of Jesus Christ.

Platt claims that American Christians "are settling for a Christianity that revolves around catering to ourselves when the central message of Christianity is actually about abandoning ourselves."[27]

In following Jesus, we continually learn the art of denying ourselves.

When the grace of God flows into our lives to cover our weaknesses, we rid ourselves of the lie that we don't really need God's help, and we realize we aren't the answer to the world's problems. While God has given us spiritual gifts that are unique to us, we understand that we can do far more when we join other talented, gifted people.

IN FOLLOWING JESUS, WE CONTINUALLY LEARN THE ART OF DENYING OURSELVES.

We don't thrive when we're isolated. Getting up, going to work, driving home, shutting our garage and turning on the TV before falling asleep—and doing the same thing the next day and the next—is becoming more common for many individuals. Introverts and extroverts are wired very differently, but no matter which one you are, you're made for relationships. We weren't created to make it on our own. We need Jesus, and we need each other. He had real, genuine relationships and cared for others, and He invites us to follow His example.

CHALLENGE

GATHER WITH OTHERS TODAY

Your options could include hosting a dinner, going on a fun outing, studying the Bible, or even discussing today's challenge and talking about how to gather together in the future. You could plan a group project to make a difference in your community.

Which one did you choose?

_____

_____

_____

_____

_____

_____

_____

_____

_____

_____

11/40

DAY 12

COMMIT TO ONE

Thomas Frank, an entrepreneur from Boulder, Colorado, wanted to be more productive, so he set up a strict schedule. He decided he needed to wake up earlier, so he set his alarm for 5:55 AM. As an added incentive, he programmed his Twitter account to automatically send a tweet that says:

@TOMFRANKLY

It's 6:10, and I'm not up because I'm lazy! Reply to this for $5 via PayPal (limit 5), assuming my alarm didn't malfunction.[28]

That's extreme accountability!

As we explore a 40-day challenge to make the five keystone habits our own, it's important to find ways to be accountable.

Do you have a friend or a mentor who could help you?

Today, some Christian leaders find themselves in the headlines because of moral failures. In fact, it seems like an epidemic! It's important to know that there are many more who never make headlines because they live a consistent, morally upright life.

One of the most well-respected disciples of Jesus was Billy Graham. He's famous for what's called the "Billy Graham Rule," which he instituted to protect his relationships with women. His rule was to never be alone with any woman who wasn't his wife, Ruth. His commitment may seem very old-fashioned, but it certainly worked for him. There was never a hint of scandal. In fact, he was a role model for all Christian leaders.

His son Franklin talks about a specific time when it would have been easy to compromise on this rule:

> *"I remember a time when Hillary Clinton, when she was the first lady of Arkansas, wanted to have Daddy come over to the Governor's Mansion for lunch, in order to talk to him. And he said, 'I'd be glad to meet you for lunch, but it would be at a public place and I'll have to have one of my associates with me, so it's not just the two of us having lunch together.'"*[29]

Billy Graham had a profound ministry to women, but these personal connections were always in the presence of someone else or in a public place. His commitment protected the women as well as himself from any rumors of scandal. He lived almost 100 years with a good reputation because of his rule. He was also transparent with his team and expected other team members to follow his example.

As a parent, I try to teach my kids what's appropriate and what's not. While they are under my roof, I'm committed to give them encouragement, discipline, teaching, and rebuke when it's needed. However, I make mistakes . . . plenty of them. Who is holding me accountable? The choices that adults make, myself included, aren't always right, and we need someone to speak into our lives to help us become greater followers of Jesus. If that's my goal, I need someone to help me to see things that I can't always see myself.

Sometimes, right and wrong are easy to see, but I encounter plenty of moments when a choice isn't clear. All of us have blind spots, and I need people who love me enough to tell me the truth about mine. Do you have someone like that in your life?

We can learn a lot about accountability from the recovery community, specifically from Alcoholics Anonymous (AA). This incredible program has a rich history, and today includes more than 115,000 groups worldwide, about half of them in the U.S., with over two million members.[30]

One of the main reasons for its effectiveness is the accountability built into it, in the frequency and availability of meetings, and in pairing each person with a sponsor. While statistics are somewhat hard to measure because of the commitment to anonymity, we can see that frequency and availability make a difference.

The more frequent the A.A. meetings the better, but a report from the *American Journal of Alcohol Abuse* showed that at least one meeting a week is required for positive results. The study showed that over 70% of those attending 12-Step groups weekly for about two years were still sober, but those who attended less than weekly had results that were similar to those who never attended any meetings.[31]

The availability of sponsors is also a vital part of how A.A. works, and numerous studies demonstrate that sponsorship significantly increases the probability of continued sobriety. An article from the *Psychology of Addictive Behaviors* reported that participants with sponsors who have attended A.A. for three months were three times more likely to have abstained from alcohol when compared to those without a sponsor.[32]

Showing up consistently and having someone to talk to make the difference in the goal of staying sober.

These same two things, consistency and having someone to talk with, can make an incredible difference in your life, too.

Christian community, when it's at its best, gives me the opportunity to talk to someone consistently, to share my heart and my struggles, and to hear God's words of forgiveness when I have fallen short.

James, the brother of Jesus, encourages us:

> **"Therefore confess your sins to each other and pray for each other so that you may be healed. The prayer of a righteous person is powerful and effective." James 5:16**

Every person struggles with something, and all of us need to be able to consistently talk with someone who will hear us, challenge us, assure us of forgiveness, and pray for us.

In trying to be the greatest follower of Jesus that I can be, I want to make sure that I continue to live in integrity. I was recently challenged to find an accountability partner. I looked at my friends and found someone who is on a similar trajectory. I put myself in a vulnerable position and asked him if he would be my accountability partner. I told him about my desire to have integrity in my private life, my family, and my church, and I explained that I needed his help to ensure I was on the right track. Initially asking him to hold me accountable felt a little weird, and when we met the first few times, it felt awkward. I wondered, "*Can I really tell him everything?*"

We came up with four questions that he asks me each week:

 How were your rhythms with God in the last week?

 How are your relationships in your family?

 Did you look at anything you shouldn't have looked at last week?

 Would your wife say anything different to your answers to the first three questions?

Each time I answer these questions, we have great conversations, and it's a two-way street. We listen, we encourage, we challenge, and then we pray. It's an incredibly refreshing time.

CHALLENGE

BE ACCOUNTABLE

Ask someone you trust to be your accountability partner for the rest of *Being Challenge*. Be specific about what you would like this person to do, for instance: text you once a day, meet weekly, ask you these four questions, or celebrate wins with you. This person needs to be available for periodic check-ins and someone you're willing to share your heart with. For some, this could be the most difficult of all of the challenges in these 40 days because it requires us to be honest and vulnerable.

ACCOUNTABILITY PARTNER AGREEMENT

What is the habit you want to work on? _____

How often will you check-in? _____

What would you like this person to do if you're struggling?

_____

_____

How long will you meet? _____

How will you celebrate at the end?

_____

_____

12/40

KEYSTONE HABIT 2:

STUD
SCRIP

DAY 13

FINDING IDENTITY IN SCRIPTURE

One of the things that amazes me about Jesus is His dedication to His mission. He knew who He was and why He came, and His purpose never wavered, even in the face of fierce opposition. I'll never understand how Jesus could be both fully God and fully man at the same time, but one of the clearest times when His humanity was on display was in the Garden of Gethsemane. It was in this moment that Jesus prayed this prayer:

> **"'Father, if you are willing, take this cup from me; yet not my will, but yours be done.' An angel from heaven appeared to him and strengthened him. And being in anguish, he prayed more earnestly, and his sweat was like drops of blood falling to the ground." Luke 22:42–44**

"The cup" represents divine judgment. For us to be forgiven, Jesus had to bear the judgment our sins deserve. He was preparing to die the death we should have died. As He faced the weight of all the world's sins, it's no wonder that He wanted to run away! But He didn't. Even in anguish, He trusted the Father. His death was the reason He came, and going to the cross was the fulfillment of His purpose. As a human being, He wanted to find another way—any other way! But He was obedient to the point of death.

Jesus knew His purpose and why He was here. He was the Son of God who came into the world to live a perfect, sinless life, and offer His body as a sacrifice for us.

Because of His great love for His Father and for you and me, He was willing to endure the excruciating agony that was central to His calling.

Do you know who you are? One of the biggest problems in the world is that many of us spend far more time listening to the lies of the enemy than to the truth of the gospel.

For the rest of today's devotion, I want to open the Scriptures and remind you of your identity. God made you. Since He made you, He gets to declare who you are. He has the ultimate naming rights for you.

> **"Through him all things were made; without him nothing was made that has been made." John 1:3**

And not only did God make you, but God loves you. How do I know this? Look at the lengths He went to show you His love:

> **"For God so loved the world that he gave his one and only Son, that whoever believes in him shall not perish but have eternal life."**
> **John 3:16**

The Father considers you to be so valuable that He gave His one and only Son to die in your place. God must really love you! He did all of this so that you would become His child:

> **"See what great love the Father has lavished on us, that we should be called children of God! And that is what we are!" 1 John 3:1**

Through Jesus' sacrifice, you become a child of God. As His child, you're given the incredible privilege to represent Him. You are chosen by God and sent into the world to make a difference.

> **"But you are a chosen people, a royal priesthood, a holy nation, God's special possession, that you may declare the praises of him who called you out of darkness into his wonderful light. Once you were not a people, but now you are the people of God; once you had not received mercy, but now you have received mercy." 1 Peter 2:9–10**

You are His special possession. The word actually means "treasure." As God's treasure, you have countless opportunities to demonstrate His character and tell others about Him.

> **"For we are co-workers in God's service!" 1 Corinthians 3:9**

Your efforts have eternal impact! In everything you do—relationships with family and friends, work, hobbies, and everything else—you can live a life of purpose by living with love and integrity and sharing the story of Jesus with people. Even when you mess up, you can know that your identity with God is secure because it's eternal and unconditional. Even when you get it wrong, you can be sure that God forgives you and nothing will separate you from Him.

> **"In all these things we are more than conquerors through him who loved us. For I am convinced that neither death nor life, neither angels nor demons, neither the present nor the future, nor any powers, neither height nor depth, nor anything else in all creation, will be able to separate us from the love of God that is in Christ Jesus our Lord." Romans 8:37–39**

ONE OF THE BIGGEST PROBLEMS IN THE WORLD IS THAT MANY OF US SPEND FAR MORE TIME LISTENING TO THE LIES OF THE ENEMY THAN TO THE TRUTH OF THE GOSPEL.

You might want to shout, "Are you serious? Nothing can separate us?" Yes, that's right. You are more than a conqueror. We don't measure our success by the world's standards. Instead, you are a super-conqueror with God. And as you go out with God, and conquer with Him, you can live a life filled with these characteristics:

"But the fruit of the Spirit is love, joy, peace, patience kindness, goodness, faithfulness, gentleness and self-control." Galatians 5:22–23

As we walk with God, the Holy Spirit increasingly produces these qualities in us. Why would anyone choose to live any other way? Is all of this too good to be true? Will the hammer drop sooner or later? Will there be a bad end to this story? No, the end is even better than the beginning!

"Praise be to the God and Father of our Lord Jesus Christ! In his great mercy he has given us new birth into a living hope through the resurrection of Jesus Christ from the dead, and into an inheritance that can never perish, spoil or fade. This inheritance is kept in heaven for you." 1 Peter 1:3–4

Your inheritance will never perish, spoil, or fade . . . Wow! It *does* sound too good to be true! Except it *is* true.

The Scriptures have a lot to say about who you are in God's sight. These are just a few verses that describe your identity as God's loved, forgiven, accepted child. You have an incredibly loving God! This doesn't guarantee that life will be easy. It certainly wasn't for Jesus, and He was the Son of God! But knowing Him, loving Him, and being used by Him is the life I want. And it's the life promised to you and all who believe.

C H A L L E N G E

TARGET PRACTICE

Assess how well you master this particular habit by drawing an arrow to where you believe you currently fall with this habit. If bullseye on the target represents mastery of this habit and each outer ring represents more improvement needed, where would you rate yourself?

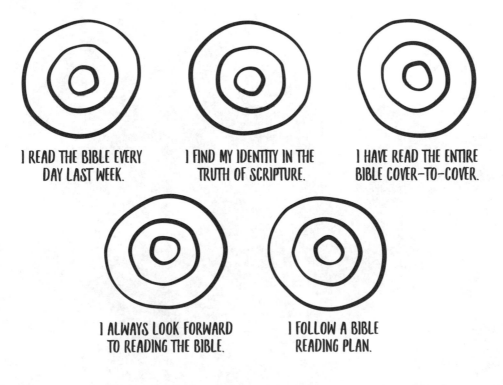

I READ THE BIBLE EVERY
DAY LAST WEEK.

I FIND MY IDENTITY IN THE
TRUTH OF SCRIPTURE.

I HAVE READ THE ENTIRE
BIBLE COVER-TO-COVER.

I ALWAYS LOOK FORWARD
TO READING THE BIBLE.

I FOLLOW A BIBLE
READING PLAN.

Based on the marked targets, where is your greatest opportunity for growth?

13/40

DAY 14

THE FOUR Rs OF STUDYING SCRIPTURE

Over the years, many people have offered great ideas about ways we can study the Scriptures. To keep things simple, I want to borrow four Rs from Rick Warren's bestselling book, *The Purpose Driven Life*.

He says you can read it, research it, remember it, and reflect on it.[33] Let's briefly look at each one.

READ IT

As you will discover on Day 17, for most of the church's history, the Scriptures weren't in the languages of the vast majority of people. Only the priests and a few wealthy, educated people were able to read the Bible in Latin. Now, it's available to billions of people in their native languages, but there's a different problem: less than a quarter of Christians have a plan when it comes to reading Scripture, and many only hear the Bible when it is read aloud at church.[34]

I was one of those people. In my early years as a believer, I opened the Bible at random and read whatever was there. Before long, I knew where the Gospels and Paul's letters were, so I made sure to flip it open there. To be sure, God used those times of reading, but I'm pretty sure He taught me in spite of my method, not because of it.

I've learned to follow a plan and ask someone to hold me accountable. The seasons when I've had a clear plan of what I'm reading, how much I'm reading, and when I'm reading are the times when I've felt most connected to God. Spending just 15 minutes a day, a very small portion of time, is enough time to read through the entire Bible in a year! For more steps on how to make a plan and stick with it, see the Final Challenge on page 264.

RESEARCH IT

There are many different methods to research the Bible, but the key difference between reading and researching is asking questions while you read. Many find it helpful to journal and jot down questions and answers. Before long, we see patterns and make connections. We understand and appreciate the main themes and see truths in context, and we can make it more personal.

As you research, you may jot down how a verse or paragraph applies to your current situation. Asking the who, what, why, where, when, and how questions will give you greater insight.

When I slow down and research God's Word, I've often been amazed that I can read a passage I've read multiple times, but it takes on a different application in that particular point in my life.

REMEMBER IT

As I'm reading and researching, I highlight some verses in my Bible, and I commit some of them to memory.

In the digital age, I'm a little worried that our ability to memorize is being neglected. A recent study showed that half of Europeans wouldn't be able to get in touch with their children or their office, and one third wouldn't know how to get in touch with their spouse without their cell phones.[35] It wasn't that long ago that we memorized phone numbers that were important to us. (I still remember the phone number of my favorite Chinese takeout restaurant from my high school days.) Your memory is like a muscle: the more you use it, the stronger it becomes. You may think you "can't memorize" Scripture, but that's not true. You probably can recite the lyrics of songs you love, and maybe even your entire playlist! If you can do that, you can certainly memorize verses in the Bible.

It has always been important for people to internalize God's truth. God gave the Israelites this encouragement: **"These commandments that I give you today are to be on your hearts. Impress them on your children. Talk about them when you sit at home and when you walk along the road, when you lie down and when you get up. Tie them as symbols on your hands and bind them on your foreheads. Write them on the doorframes of your houses and on your gates." Deuteronomy 6:6–9**

Jesus modeled this practice for us. As I mentioned earlier, 10% of all that Jesus said was quoted from the Old Testament.

It's very helpful to build the list of passages we've memorized so they cover important topics like God's love, our identity, His purposes for us, forgiveness, and how to relate to others (to name only a few). By memorizing God's Word, we bring God's truth out of the pages of a book and into our hearts and minds.

REFLECT ON IT

After reading, researching, and remembering, don't stop; reflect on what you've just taken in. The Bible uses the word "meditation" to describe reflection. King

BY MEMORIZING
GOD'S WORD,
WE BRING GOD'S
TRUTH OUT OF
THE PAGES OF A
BOOK AND INTO
OUR HEARTS
AND MINDS.

David was described as a man after God's own heart because he loved to reflect on God's Word. David says this in Psalm 119:97: **"Oh, how I love your law! I meditate on it all day long."**

Not long ago, I experienced a series of hard knocks. I felt incredibly inadequate and extremely overwhelmed. During that time, a particular verse stood out to me. I memorized it and reflected on it, saying it over and over. It was from the prophet Jeremiah: **"Ah, Sovereign Lord, you have made the heavens and the earth by your great power and outstretched arm. Nothing is too hard for you." Jeremiah 32:17.** It was the perfect verse that I needed to read, remember, and reflect on. For a few weeks I repeated the phrase, "Nothing is too hard for You." As I declared this truth again and again, I could feel my fear and worry being replaced with joy and delight. This is what reflecting on God's Word can do for you.

We'll speak much more about meditation on Day 33.

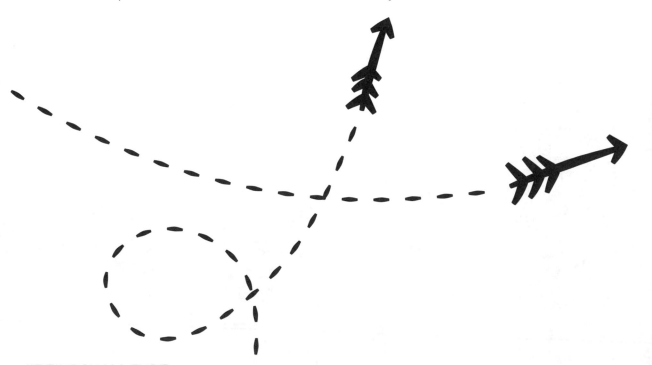

CHALLENGE

RANKING THE FOUR Rs

Rank the Four Rs from easiest to hardest for you: Read, Research, Remember, and Reflect.

EASIEST

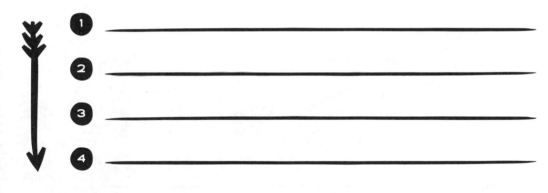

1 _____

2 _____

3 _____

4 _____

HARDEST

What makes your top choice the easiest and what makes your bottom choice the hardest?

_____

_____

Over the next four days, the challenges will focus on the four Rs!

14/40

DAY 15

KNOWING WHO YOU ARE INFLUENCES THE WAY YOU LIVE.

This is the golden age of self-discovery. Most people can tell you their top five strengths according to their Strengthsfinder's Assessment; they know their number on the Enneagram (I'm a number 8 by the way, which is "The Challenger." It makes sense, right? After all, I'm writing a book with the word "challenge" in it!); they can tell you if they're a Golden Retriever, a Beaver, a Lion, or an Otter, their love language, and which Disney character they're like according to a Facebook quiz.

Personality tests and online assessments can be helpful, but it's far more helpful to look to the One who created you—God himself. The Bible does many things for us, but today I want to focus on how God's truth communicates our true identity as God's child. We find who God is and who we are when we study Scripture.

In fact, the only place to find your true identity is God's Word.

This isn't a secondary topic. We won't be able to practice the five keystone habits if we aren't convinced that we belong to God.

When I spoke on this topic, someone asked a very interesting question: "Do our habits shape our identity, or does our identity shape our habits?" I want to argue the answer is yes . . . both/and. Here's why:

The word "identity" was originally derived from the Latin words *essentitas,* which means being, and *identitem*, which means repeatedly. Your identity is literally your "repeated beingness."[36]

Your identity and your habits are completely intertwined. What does this mean? Your habits shape your identity, and your identity shapes your habits.

It's not healthy to find your primary identity in the world's standards of success, beauty, and popularity. And you can't find your identity by looking more deeply into yourself. That's the most common form of goal setting. People try to determine what they want to do, but their questions are entirely self-focused: "What do I want to do? What are my ambitions and my dreams for my future?" But here's the truth: when we focus on ourselves, we never discover our purpose or our identity.

If I handed you something I made, maybe an invention you'd never seen before, you wouldn't know its purpose, and the invention itself wouldn't be able to tell you. Only the creator or the owner's manual could reveal its purpose.

"It is God who directs the lives of his creatures; everyone's life is in his power." Job 12:10 GNT

Only the One who made you gets to decide who you are. Until you understand that, your life will never make sense. You'll try all kinds of things to be somebody, but you'll be living under a false identity. This is a revolutionary concept for people who have tried so hard to find meaning in achievement, prestige, titles, possessions, approval, or comfort—or a combination of these things. But in fact, no matter how much of these things we possess, they can't fill our hearts. They may give momentary pleasure, but soon they leave us empty and desperate... and confused.

People have dreams of what will give them ultimate fulfillment, and they usually pursue a spouse, a house, a career, a nice car, enough in a savings account, and great vacations, but even then, they're still not satisfied. Why? Because we were made to be God's children, and until we step into our identity as children of God, we'll never be the people we were meant to be.

Blaise Pascal, a 17th century mathematician, philosopher, and theologian, observed:

> *"Not only do we know God through Jesus Christ, but we only know ourselves through Jesus Christ. We only know life and death through Jesus Christ. Apart from Jesus we cannot know the meaning of our life, the meaning of our death, the meaning of God, or the meaning of ourselves. It is only in Christ."*

Only one being has the right to stamp an identity on you—and it's not you, the kids at school, your boss, your friends, your spouse, or your mom or dad—it's God. You can pursue another identity, but you undoubtedly find yourself empty, angry, and frustrated. As Pascal said, true meaning comes only when our identity is rooted firmly in Christ.

When people consider their life's purpose, many begin with their careers. I think it's much better to start with an idea of what kind of person we want to become. The who comes before the do. Nothing shapes your habits more than your sense of identity.

YOUR HABITS
SHAPE YOUR
IDENTITY, AND
YOUR IDENTITY
SHAPES YOUR
HABITS.

You step into your identity as a child of God only through faith.

Habits may be something you do, but faith isn't something you do. It's a gift that only God can give. Even though this book focuses on the habits of Jesus, I want to be very clear: While Jesus provided an example of the way we're called to live, if you're only looking to Jesus as your example, you will be crushed by the expectations. Many people make this mistake. They see Jesus as their model, but before long, they realize they've fallen far short of His love, wisdom, self-control, and compassion. We simply can't live like Him! To be sure, Jesus is an example, but He's much more than that: He's our Savior and Lord. He knows that even our best efforts fall short, so He reminds us of His forgiveness, and He assures us that His purpose for us remains true and strong. We live by faith in His provision of forgiveness and purpose.

How did the disciples, most of whom ran when Jesus was arrested, become dynamic leaders of the new movement of Christ followers? Because God gave them the faith to believe. How do we have faith? Through God.

"So faith comes from hearing, and hearing through the word of Christ."
Romans 10:17 ESV

God's Word changes us because faith comes through the Scriptures. When the Good News of Jesus is presented and His death and resurrection is preached, read, taught, said, and demonstrated, the Holy Spirit gives us eyes to see and hearts to believe. As our faith in Jesus grows, we'll be saying things like this: "I want to be a greater follower of Jesus Christ, and that's why it's important to develop habits that help me be more like Him." My faith shapes my habits, and it begins with knowing the One who made me. I discover more about Him and about myself when I study the Scriptures.

C H A L L E N G E

FOLLOW A BIBLE READING PLAN

If you don't have one, find one and start today! A Bible reading plan is a great way for you to stay disciplined in the area of studying Scripture.

To be helpful we've provided a link at www.beingchallenge.com/bibleplans that can point you to many great options.

Our suggestion is to pick one that will last at least 30 days! After picking a plan, please share which plan you are reading with at least one friend that can help keep you accountable.

MY BIBLE READING PLAN:

_____

15/40

DAY 16

NOT A BLIND FAITH

So far, we've seen how we find our identity in our study of the Scriptures. We then reminded ourselves what the Scriptures say about us. But can we trust that the words we are studying are actually the true words of God? After all, the Bible was written long ago by many different authors. Today, there is a debate about the authenticity and reliability of the Bible.

Bart Ehrman, author of *Misquoting Jesus* and *Jesus Interrupted*, has also been featured on *The Daily Show* and *The Colbert Report*. When he was asked about the story of Jesus, he insisted, "There's not a single scholar on the face of the Earth that buys any of it."[37]

Bill Maher, a popular comedian, claims, "The Bible looks like it started out as a game of Mad Libs."[38]

How do you respond to statements like these?

Our natural response is to fight back and argue. While I believe there's a time and place for debates, I want to remind you that the reason we believe the Bible is truly God's Word isn't because of its reliability or credibility, but rather, because the Holy Spirit has worked faith in us. There is no reasoning, argument, statistics, or proof that I can give you that will make you say, "Yes, now I know for certain the Bible is true." Only the Holy Spirit can do that as He opens our eyes to the truth that's in

God's Word. <u>We believe in the Bible because the Holy Spirit produces faith in us to believe.</u>

Here's why this is a better response than to debate the skeptics:

Some Christians feel the need to defend God and His Word at every point, but they have to speculate on some things they don't really know for sure. When they insist they're certain, and the unbeliever shoots holes in their argument, they look foolish, and their misguided attempt to defend the authority of the Bible does more harm than good.

We need equally strong doses of humility and wisdom. Can we admit that it's hard to answer some questions about our faith? Over the years I've had to admit I don't have all the scientific answers, such as how dinosaurs came into the story, or how Jonah could have lived in the stomach of a whale for several days (that's a hard story for me to wrap my head around). Even the crux of our faith—the virgin birth of the Son of God who would die and miraculously rise from the dead—can't be easily explained.

But my unanswered questions don't make me feel stupid. The Holy Spirit gives us faith to believe, but it's not a blind faith.

Lee Strobel, a former journalist, investigated the reliability of the Bible and its claims about Jesus Christ. He documents this journey in his book, *The Case for Christ*. I highly recommend this book if you have questions about the legitimacy of the Bible and the person of Jesus Christ.

As we explore the Bible and first century historical accounts, one of the things we see over and over is the evidence that Jesus really did live, He really did die, and He really did rise from the dead.

The resurrection of Jesus ensures us that we don't have a blind faith. The resurrection changes everything. The scholars and scientists who have scoffed at the intelligence of Christians can't explain away the resurrection.

On Day 2 when we introduced the topic of studying the Bible, we talked about how Jesus opened the Scriptures and explained them to the disciples. But this time, look at what it says: **"Then Jesus opened their minds so they could understand the Scriptures." Luke 24:45.** Their minds were opened.

This wasn't the first time Jesus had opened the Scriptures to them. He had been teaching them for the past three years, so what was the difference this time? Why were their minds suddenly opened at this moment?

The resurrection.

They knew the Scriptures all along, but without Jesus' resurrection, they didn't have understanding.

His resurrection changes people and inspires them to do good. Truthfully, there are stacks of books about developing good habits. You don't have to go through this 40-day challenge to realize the value of good habits. But the understanding, the why, the foundational, earth-shifting piece that changes everything is Jesus' resurrection.

Look at what the apostle Paul writes:

"For the message of the cross is foolishness to those who are perishing, but to us who are being saved it is the power of God." 1 Corinthians 1:18

The historical evidence of the cross and the resurrection forms the foundation of our faith. We believe Jesus came out of the tomb alive and transformed because the Holy Spirit gives us the faith to believe. And the same Holy Spirit gives us the faith to believe that the Bible really is God's Word.

Am I foolish for believing this? I don't think so, but others might look at me that way. Science was my worst subject in school, but I know that a number of "certainties" in science have been disproven. Theories like the Earth being flat; the Earth being at the center of the universe; the atom being the smallest particle; that all matter was made up of four elements: earth, air, fire, and water; the idea that life could suddenly emerge from inanimate objects; that heavier objects fall faster than lighter objects; and many others. At different times, all of these ideas were considered to be facts, but they've all been disproven. We can be sure that some of today's scientific "facts" will be disproven at some time in the future.

We need to spend less time debating about the specific, hard to understand things of the Bible, and spend more time talking about the resurrection of Jesus Christ. It's a fact, and this fact moves people to believe in the God of the Bible.

A proper response isn't to argue with those who don't believe, but simply to thank God for opening our minds to understand and to pray that those who don't have faith will one day believe.

And here's the faith I have today: The same God who is powerful enough to create the world and defy the laws of nature by raising Jesus from the dead is also capable of preserving His Word over centuries.

The principle message of the Bible has never changed. The Scriptures, from beginning to end, describe the wonderful, sweeping plan of a loving, powerful God. It's the message about the Son of God who lived the perfect life we can't live and died the death we should have died. He died a horrible death when our punishment fell on Him. Only by His stripes that He suffered on the cross are we forgiven and healed. All of this was predicted in the Old Testament, and in Jesus, it all came true. God cares about us so much that He sent not only His Son, but also His words that help us walk with confidence every day of our lives!

The resurrection changes everything. One of the tools to help us in our research is called a "concordance," which records every mention in the Bible of a particular word. Today, as we have focused on the resurrection, your challenge will be to look at the accounts of the word "resurrection" to help you understand and believe this life-changing, earth-shattering event!

If you enjoy this type of study, you may want to do a similar word study on grace, faith, hope, love, joy, peace, patience, etc. sometime in the future.

CHALLENGE

RESURRECTION RESEARCH

Acts is a historical book in the New Testament that describes the ascension of Jesus and the start of the early church. As you look at these, it may be helpful to read the verses around them to see the context.

ACTS 1:22	ACTS 4:33	ACTS 23:6-8
ACTS 2:32	ACTS 17:18	ACTS 24:15
ACTS 4:2	ACTS 17:32	ACTS 24:21

Based on your reading, what did you learn about the resurrection?

_____

_____

Do you believe in Jesus' resurrection from the dead?

_____

If the resurrection of Jesus is real, how does it matter to you and your choices?

_____

_____

If you still struggle to believe the resurrection of Jesus, what's holding you back? What are some questions you'd like to have answered?

_____

_____

16/40

DAY 17

KNOW THE TRUTH

Two historical events that happened close to each other revolutionized culture. Before the invention of the printing press and the Protestant Reformation led by Martin Luther, the Bible was communicated only in Latin, which was incomprehensible to most people who attended church. Luther translated the Bible into German, and other theologians translated it into many other languages. The printing press made it available to far more people, not just the priests or the elite. The Reformers were then able to correct many errors that had been communicated for centuries.

Many leaders in the church were afraid of regular people reading the Bible because they might come up with wrong interpretations.

Fast-forward to today: believers have embraced many different interpretations of the Scriptures, which has led to many different denominations. It appears that the fears of the past have become a reality, and yet, it's undoubtedly a very good thing that far more people have the Bible in their own language. God has called each of us to follow Him, and He has given us His Word. We shouldn't discourage anyone from reading and studying the Scriptures.

Today, we have the Bible in many different formats and in many different languages. As early as 2025, the Bible is on track to be translated into every language throughout the world. Many of us carry around the Bible on our phones in our pockets. We can read it, listen to it, and study it in many different ways. There are study Bibles, journaling Bibles, kids' Bibles, teens' Bibles, etc.

Here's the problem: How do you know which interpretation or version is right? How do you know which one is speaking God's truth most clearly?

We live in a postmodern world where many believe everyone's truth is equally valid, but that can't be right. Two competing versions of truth are, at least to some degree, mutually exclusive. They may both be wrong, but they can't both be right. Where can we turn for clarity?

The Bible contains truth. Timeless truth.

The Bible is truth, but not every interpretation of the Bible is truth.

Can you recognize truth? A spiritual battle is taking place right now. God is speaking truth, and the devil is speaking lies. In fact, the devil is known as "the father of lies." The traditional picture of the devil, a red dragon-like creature with pointy ears and a pitchfork, isn't helpful. If this is what the devil looked like, we'd know to run away. A more accurate picture of the devil is that he is very attractive, even that he comes disguised as "an angel of light." He uses enough truth so we let our guard down, and then he twists it into a lie.

If I were the devil, I would attack pastors and leaders first and foremost. I'm not encouraging you to doubt your pastor, but you should always test what your pastor says.

The apostle John reminds us of this:

"Beloved, do not believe every spirit, but test the spirits to see whether they are from God, because many false prophets have gone out into the world." 1 John 4:1

Do you know God's Word well enough to distinguish between truths and lies? When I preach, I tell my church that they should *listen* to what I say, but they should always *test* what I say. I'm sure I've unintentionally said some things that were wrong. Similarly, you should *test* what you're reading in this book. How do we test anyone's teaching? First, we look at the context of the passage to see if what the teacher is saying is consistent with the wider text. Sometimes (often?), people pull a verse out of context and try to make it say something the writer didn't intend. Second, we look at a trustworthy study Bible to see what godly scholars say about the passage. (It's helpful to know the particular point of view of the study Bible you're using. You can Google it to find out.) Third, talk to someone who has a different point of view to see the passage from another angle. Sometimes, a different perspective helps us make sense of the first person's teaching. And fourth, determine whether the teaching is consistent with the truth you've been taught before. Be wary of "new truth" that promises more than God intends to deliver.

I'm hopeful that during this week, you'll make studying Scripture personal and powerful enough that it will give you the ability to distinguish truth from lies. As you study over weeks, months, and years, you'll develop a spiritual "sixth sense" that enables you to detect errors, or maybe inconsistencies, in a teacher's message. None of us get it right all the time, but the pastors and teachers I respect love God's Word and strive to teach it with power, integrity, and clarity.

THE BIBLE IS TRUTH, BUT NOT EVERY INTERPRETATION OF THE BIBLE IS TRUTH.

The truth is always centered in Jesus. Do you know the voice of Jesus? In speaking of himself, Jesus declares that He is the Good Shepherd:

"He calls his own sheep by name and leads them out. When he has brought out all his own, he goes on ahead of them, and his sheep follow him because they know his voice. But they will never follow a stranger; in fact, they will run away from him because they do not recognize a stranger's voice." John 10:3–5

Followers of Jesus are able to recognize His voice and run from the voice of the enemy. As we follow the voice of Jesus, He welcomes us into life to the fullest!

CHALLENGE

BIBLE MEMORY

In our challenge today, we're focusing on the importance of *remembering*. Memorizing Scripture is a great way to build a foundation of truth. Memorize a new verse for the week. Write it on a notecard or create a new wallpaper for your phone with the verse on it.

Write out your memory verse here:

_____

_____

_____

_____

_____

_____

If you are looking for a verse to memorize, let me suggest five:

PSALM 136:1   **PROVERBS 3:5**   **JOHN 3:16-17**

ROMANS 5:8:   **EPHESIANS 2:8-9:**

If you'd like to memorize more Bible verses, I encourage you to check out this page: www.beingchallenge.com/memoryverses.

17/40

DAY 18

YOU ARE WHAT YOU EAT

Yesterday we talked about knowing God's Word, which is vital to our relationship with God. Jesus certainly knew the Scriptures, and we will benefit if we imitate Him in this matter.

But it's not just about _knowing_ God's Word.

It's about _being changed_ by God's Word.

The great pastor and evangelist D.L. Moody once said, "The Bible was not given to increase our knowledge but to change our lives."[39] As I've heard my dad say many times, "The Bible provides information, but even more – transformation."

The reason we study the Scriptures so diligently is because God's Word contains truth that's transformative for today . . . and every day. The Scriptures weren't written only to help us attain eternal life someday in the future, but also, to give us wisdom and strength today, right now, in our relationships with the people around us and in our current situations.

It's crucial—eternally important—that we learn certain things, but some information isn't important even if it's interesting.

The inventor Thomas Edison had a challenging test for employees who wanted to work for him. They had to answer 146 random questions. Here is a small sampling of the questions applicants were asked. See how well you would do!

1. What is the greatest known depth of the ocean?

2. Who invented the cotton gin?

3. What place is the greatest distance below sea level?

4. Who discovered the Pacific Ocean?

5. Is Australia greater in area than Greenland?

6. How did the United States acquire Louisiana?

7. Who was Solon?

If you're like me, you would have failed the test. By the way, the answers are in the endnotes.[40]

Edison gave this test because he valued employees who could memorize large amounts of information. While knowing the answers to Edison's questions might help you win $50 at a local trivia night or beat James Holzhauer on *Jeopardy*, I'm not sure it matters if you know how we got Louisiana (unless you're a student and it's on the test).

However, the more we know, study, and memorize God's Word, the more it will sustain us through the ups and downs of life.

Pastor Rick Warren says, "God's Word generates life, creates faith, produces change, frightens the devil, causes miracles, heals hurts, builds character, transforms circumstances, imparts joy, overcomes adversity, defeats temptation, infuses hope, releases power, cleanses our minds, brings things into being, and guarantees our future ... You should consider it as essential to your life as food."[41]

Jesus explained, **"People need more than bread for life; they must feed on every word of God." Matthew 4:4**

As we consume the Scriptures, it transforms us. And when we're transformed by God, we help change the world.

How does God's Word transform us?

Practically, studying God's Word is a keystone habit in my life. I've found that the days that I study the Word of God, I'm naturally calmer, more patient, and gracious. The more I'm in God's Word, the more I become like Christ. Luke, the historian of the early church, wrote: **"God's ... gracious Word can make you into what he wants you to be and give you everything you could possibly need." Acts 20:32 MSG** The more I consume God's Word, the more I think like Jesus, pray like Jesus, and act like Jesus in my day-to-day relationships and obligations.

The reason His Word changes me is because it's Good News! The more I dig into God's Word, the more I discover His great love for me. It's ultimately God's kindness that gives me the desire and the power to change.

I'm very grateful for the grace He's given to me. Reading about His grace fills my heart and encourages me to extend grace to others.

AS WE CONSUME
THE SCRIPTURES,
IT TRANSFORMS US.
AND WHEN WE'RE
TRANSFORMED
BY GOD, WE HELP
CHANGE THE WORLD.

I'm amazed that He would choose someone like me to live with a God-inspired purpose. God's grace not only forgives me but restores me, a realization that helps me develop a greater desire to serve those in need.

I'm stunned that God would give His one and only Son to die for me. Seeing God's generosity helps me become more generous in how I act toward others.

I have a wonderful hope that Jesus will come back for me someday. This promise shows me that "the final chapter" is a glorious one, which helps me maintain courage in difficult times and learn that true joy isn't found in circumstances.

If God's Word is working in us and changing us, we will join Him on mission to help others.

In the Old Testament, God gave Ezekiel His words on a scroll and had Ezekiel literally eat the scroll. The imagery is fascinating. It tells me that when we eat God's words and digest them, they become part of us, nourishing and empowering us to do whatever God directs us to do.

In countless experiences during hard times, I've leaned on God's Word. When I've committed to the right community, people often have brought me encouragement from the Scriptures. Hearing God's Word in a time of trouble changes me, unlike experiences of pleasure or success. You have the same opportunity. The more of God's truth you eat and digest, the stronger you'll be, and you'll make a difference for Him.

Scripture isn't meant only to be consumed; it's meant to transform.

CHALLENGE

REFLECTION TIME

Spend some time reflecting on a verse or section of Scripture. After you read it, write down what it means to you. What is God saying to you through His Word today? If you need help picking a verse or section of Scripture, look back to yesterday's challenge for some encouraging verses or visit www.beingchallenge.com/memoryverses.

_____

_____

_____

_____

_____

_____

_____

_____

_____

_____

18/40

DAY 19

GOD IS SPEAKING THROUGH THE SCRIPTURES

Imagine being in high school and getting a text that reads:

> I WAS THINKING ABOUT YOU. WE HAVEN'T SPENT MUCH TIME TOGETHER LATELY. LET'S CATCH UP ON FRIDAY NIGHT!

How would you respond if . . .

...It was from your mom or Dad?

...It was from someone you were hoping would become your best friend (or maybe your boyfriend or girlfriend)?

Being able to identify the writer makes all the difference in the world! The words have a very different meaning depending on who wrote it.

Who wrote the Bible? Was it just a group of great thinkers who called the world to live a different type of life? Or did God write it? Or is it some combination of the two? Because, depending on who wrote it, the meaning is quite different. If it is the words of God, it means much more than if it's just the words of men . . . even great men.

Let's back up and examine the Bible. In the last few days, we've talked about the importance of our identity and what the Bible says about us, but it's important, as we study Scripture, that we understand whose words we're reading.

In the Christian church, we believe in the "verbal inspiration" of the Bible, not only because the Bible teaches it, but also because God's authorship gives us confidence in what we read. One of the Bible verses that gives us insight is in the apostle Paul's second letter to Timothy:

> **"All Scripture is inspired by God and profitable for teaching, for reproof, for correction, for training in righteousness; so that the man of God may be adequate, equipped for every good work." 2 Timothy 3:16–17**

What does it mean to be "God-inspired" or, to use other translations, "God-breathed"?

Somehow (we're not exactly sure how), God interacted with these men and worked through them to provide us with His words. How did this interaction happen? Here's what we know from Scripture: To Jeremiah, God said: **"Write all the words that I have spoken to you in a book." Jeremiah 36:2.** David wrote, **"The Spirit of the Lord spoke by me and His word was on my tongue." 2 Samuel 23:2.** Peter tells us that the holy men of God spoke **"as they were moved by the Holy Spirit." 2 Peter 1:21.** Paul informs us that the things which he taught were expressed in words **"which the Holy Spirit teaches." 1 Corinthians 2:13.**

God spoke in different ways at different times to the writers of the Bible. However, they weren't just robots spouting out the words. They knew what they were doing.

Each writer used his mental powers, arranged his thoughts and arguments, chose his words, constructed his sentences, and retained his own style, and it was all directed by the Holy Spirit. The Spirit employed different types of men as His scribes—kings and peasants, fishermen and scholars, priests and prophets—making use of their unique abilities, learning, and styles of writing. The Bible teaches the fact of its inspiration, but not the "how," and there is nothing in the realm of human experience that can fully explain the inspiration of Scripture to us.

These are God's words, breathed into the lives of some great men of the faith through the Holy Spirit and recorded in their own styles for our benefit so we can hear God's voice as often as we need.

If it was great men like Moses, Peter, John, and Paul who wrote the Bible, it might be considered a great piece of literature, but it wouldn't change anybody's eternity. But if it's God's words, then it changes everything!

If it were Peter who said, **"Cast all your anxiety on me because I care for you" 1 Peter 5:7,** then you might respond, "That's nice, but seriously Peter, why do you have authority in my life to give me instructions? When hard times came, you denied Christ three times, so you're not exactly one to tell me what to do!" But if it's God who says, "Cast all your anxiety on me because I care for you," wouldn't that give you great confidence and strength? You would know that God is in charge, and He cares for you.

If it were only a human writer who said, **"I will never leave or forsake you" Hebrews 13:5,** you might get a restraining order to prevent him from stalking, but if it was God saying that, the same statement would give you hope and comfort, especially in tough times.

If it were Jeremiah who said, **"I will love you with an everlasting love" Jeremiah 31:3,** that sounds really nice, but where are you now Jeremiah? The last I heard, you were just a bullfrog and a great friend of mine. I don't know about you, but I'd rather have God be a great friend of mine. Seriously, if it's God who says He will "love you with an everlasting love," doesn't that make you feel special and important?

These are God's words, breathed into the lives of some great men of the faith through the Holy Spirit and recorded in their own styles for our benefit so we can hear God's voice as often as we need.

Almost 90% of American households contain a Bible, and the average household has three. But even among Americans who worship in church, less than half read the Bible daily, and less than a quarter have a systematic approach for reading the Bible. LifeWay Research Executive Director Scott McConnell says, "The only time most Americans hear the Bible is when someone else is reading it."[42]

WE HEAR GOD'S VOICE MOST CLEARLY WHEN WE READ THE BIBLE.

Every year, we invite people who come to our church to ask questions . . . any questions. Last year, the most common one was, "How do I hear the voice of God?"

In response, we launched a series to help people hear the voice of God. I'd love to communicate the entire series, but for now, I want to keep it very simple and remind you that if the Bible contains the very words of God, then every day, at any moment, you can open the pages and hear Him speaking to you! We hear God's voice most clearly as we read the Bible. The amazing part is that when we read these words, they actually do something in us and to us. The author of Hebrews declares to us that that these words are alive and active (Hebrews 4:12).

McConnell explains, "Scripture describes itself as 'living and effective,' according to the book of Hebrews. Those who have a habit of reading through the Bible a little each day say they have experienced this helpful, life-changing quality."

Martin Luther, the great Reformer, once said, "Therefore if you want to be certain what God in heaven thinks of you, and whether He is gracious to you, you must not seclude yourself, retire into some nook, and brood about it or seek the answer in your works or in your contemplation—all this you must banish from your heart, and you must give ear solely to the words of this Christ; for everything is revealed in Him."[43]

I hope you're eager to open the Word of God, and I'm sure that if you do, you'll be changed because the love of God will be revealed to you in the very words of God!

CHALLENGE

SHARE SCRIPTURE

This week, we've been diving into the Scriptures, but the challenge today is for you to use Scripture to encourage someone. Send an encouraging word from the Bible to all of the people in your "12." You could use text, email, or handwritten notes.

If you need help choosing a verse or a passage to share, look back at this week's challenges and Bible verses or visit www.beingchallenge.com/memoryverses.

What scripture will you share?

_____

_____

_____

_____

_____

_____

_____

_____

_____

_____

19/40

KEYSTONE HABIT 3:

PRIOR

PRAY

DAY 20

WHERE DO I GO?

A lot of people don't know what direction they're going. If you look at the movement of their lives on a map, it's filled with zigzags, twists, and turns. When we don't know the direction we ought to go, it's hard to know which habits will best serve us. The habit of prayer, which we're exploring this week, will direct us.

GPS is an incredible invention. To prevent the poaching of elephants for their tusks, investigative journalist Bryan Christy found a way to track the route of the smugglers. He commissioned a taxidermist to create two fake ivory tusks which he embedded with specially designed tracking devices. The plan worked, and the poachers were caught. Actually, Christy and his team identified all the stops from Africa to China. They discovered that the tusks were traded for arms and medicine, and that many of the park rangers were complicit in this illegal activity. It was a major victory you can chalk up to GPS.[44]

But things don't always go well with GPS. A woman in Belgium got into her car to pick up a friend at the train station. She activated her drive app to give her the best route to the station, which was about 90 miles away and probably a two-hour trip. She followed the directions. She should have gone north, but her GPS took her south and east, taking her turn-by-turn all the way to the city of Zagreb, the capital city of Croatia. In case you aren't too knowledgeable about the geography of Europe, let me explain: she was over 900 miles away from where she wanted to go!

During her escapade to pick up her friend at the train station, she stopped two times to get gas, slept for a few hours on the side of the road, and even suffered a minor car accident. It sounds crazy, but she was just following her GPS.[45]

Sometimes, even when we follow the best of the world's directions, it takes us to the wrong destination.

While we can laugh at this story, many of us are doing the same thing spiritually as this Belgian woman. We want to get to the feet of Jesus, but we're blindly following the directions of the world.

Would you let me ask a difficult but important question?

Why do we follow the directions of the world? Seriously, why do we? What are we chasing that the world offers? Some things look appealing on the outside, but following the world's directions will just make you another normal, worldly person.

Let me tell you what's normal for people:

- The average American hasn't made a new friend in the last five years.[46]
- Despite economic times booming for a decade, three out of four Americans are lonely.[47]
- 73% of people are in debt, and the average amount, excluding home, is $38,000.[48]
- 78% of people live paycheck to paycheck.[49]

- About half of marriages end in divorce in America, the sixth worst rate in the world.[50]

- In 1950, 93% of children were raised in homes with two parents; now that number is 69%.[51]

These statistics are very good reasons I'm not interested in being normal. I want to be different. I want to challenge the status quo and tell you there's a better way. Here's the life that God invites us into:

> **"Dear friends, I urge you, as foreigners and exiles, to abstain from sinful desires, which wage war against your soul. Live such good lives among the pagans that, though they accuse you of doing wrong, they may see your good deeds and glorify God on the day he visits us."**
> **1 Peter 2:11–12**

The Bible tells us that we are "foreigners" and "exiles," other translations say "aliens" and "strangers." We aren't called to be normal, but to be different. God has chosen us to be His, and He has called us to stand out as we live a life of love instead of hate, joy instead of resentment, and purpose instead of drifting. As we grow in our relationship with God, others will see, and others will glorify God . . . and eventually, heaven will have more residents!

So, be different.

But how? What does that look like?

Unless we're intentional and determined, the world will pull us in its direction.

PRAYING
GIVES ME
DIRECTION IN
A CONFUSING
WORLD.

The world has always been messy and broken, but with the conflicting messages on social media, you could make the case that the world has never been as confusing as it is right now. But God gives the gift of prayer that allows us to talk to Him at any point. We can cut through all of the confusion and chaos and communicate with the God who created us.

In the midst of a confusing world, I can go to God, and He will give me direction.

Praying gives me direction in a confusing world.

And unlike your favorite GPS navigation system, He'll never steer you in the wrong direction.

Where do I go to get this direction?

"If any of you lacks wisdom, you should ask God who gives generously to all without finding fault, and it will be given to you." James 1:5

As we develop the keystone habits of Jesus, we need to be continually directed by God through prayer.

CHALLENGE

TARGET PRACTICE

Assess how you "PRIORITIZE PRAYER" on the target images below. Use these five statements to help you:

I PRAYED EVERY DAY
LAST WEEK.

I BELIEVE IN THE POWER
OF PRAYER.

PRAYER IS THE FIRST THING
I DO IN THE MORNING.

I PRAY OFTEN AND
CONTINUALLY THROUGHOUT
THE DAY.

WHEN I NEED DIRECTION,
PRAYER IS THE FIRST
THING I DO.

Based on the marked targets, where is your greatest opportunity for growth?

_____

_____

20/40

DAY 21

FIRST RESPONSE OR LAST RESORT?

Today, I want to urge you to pray first . . . in two specific ways. Let prayer be the very first thing you do every day when you wake up, and let prayer be your first response when you face life's difficulties or demands.

Prayer ought to be a first response, not a last resort.

We see both in the life of Jesus. First, we see Jesus praying early:

> **"Very early in the morning, while it was still dark, Jesus got up, left the house and went off to a solitary place, where he prayed." Mark 1:35**

What would it look like for you to pray first thing in the morning?

Human beings value routines. We try to make individual tasks into habits as much as possible. I bet I can tell you, with pretty close accuracy, what your tomorrow morning will look like if I could have seen what you did this morning.

What is the first thing you do when you get up? The odds are very high that what you did first today you will do first tomorrow and on each normal day after that. In other words, if your alarm woke you up to day, you probably were awakened by your alarm yesterday. Or if you got up with no alarm this morning, you probably got up with no alarm yesterday, and you'll do it again tomorrow. The pattern probably holds true in your bedtime, your schedule for eating, the way you like your coffee, the kinds of food you eat, your exercise, and your habits in using social media. You probably took a shower, which is good—you may not be employed or have any friends if you don't do that every day. You probably got to work the same way and at the same time you did yesterday.

Jesus had a habit of praying early in the morning. Over the last couple of years, I've turned into a morning person. I love the quiet, the still, the calm before the busyness of the day. It's a perfect time to invite God into my day.

But there are still days I don't prioritize prayer—and by prioritize, I mean make it first. When we say, "I'll get to it when I get to it," we're not making it a priority.

The definition of priority has changed over time. In his bestselling book, *Essentialism*, Greg McKeown explains the surprising history of the word priority and how its meaning has shifted:

> *"The word priority came into the English language in the 1400s. It was singular. It meant the very first or prior thing. It stayed singular for the next five hundred years. Only in the 1900s did we pluralize the term and start talking about priorities. Illogically, we reasoned that by changing the word we could bend reality. Somehow, we would now be able to have multiple 'first' things.*
>
> *People and companies routinely try to do just that. One leader told me of this experience in a company that talked of 'Pri-1, Pri-2, Pri-3, Pri-4, and Pri-5.' This gave the impression of many things being the priority but actually meant nothing was."*[52]

To prioritize literally means to make something "the very first thing." It's something regarded as more important than anything or anyone, and it goes before other things. Is prayer that for you? Early in the morning? The first thing?

Corrie Ten Boom once said, "Don't pray when you feel like it. Have an appointment with the Lord and keep it. A man is powerful on his knees."

The second way to prioritize prayer is when life's demands and difficulties come upon us, and our first response is to pray. God is with us, and He has the power to help us in our moments of need.

"But Jesus often withdrew to lonely places and prayed." Luke 5:16

For Jesus, it wasn't just "I'll say all My prayers in the morning and get on with My day." He was in regular conversation with God all during the day.

When life's demands come my way, I sometimes forget to pray until someone asks, "Well, Zach, did you pray about it?" At that moment, I know they're right. Duh. How did I forget that? I can fall into the same trap as other Christians who spend more time talking about the power of prayer than actually praying. I don't want that to be true for me, and I'm sure you don't either.

The other day, my son Nathan wasn't feeling well on the airplane. We were worried because it was a 12-hour flight. I didn't know what to do. My worry multiplied because I realized there was nothing I could do. Then, finally, after about 10 minutes of feeling helpless, it dawned on me: "Oh yeah, I can pray." Why did it take me a few minutes? I'm not sure, but I when I remembered, I told God, "I believe You can heal Nathan and give him strength. Please do that." Before long, Nathan felt better.

PRAYER OUGHT TO BE A FIRST RESPONSE NOT A LAST RESORT.

#BEINGCHALLENGE

Was it my prayer? I don't know, but I can point to Bible verse after Bible verse that says that if we need anything, to ask God, and He will give it to us.

This means that when I'm going into a tough meeting at work, I can pray for God's Spirit to direct me. This means that before I go into the doctor's office, I can pray for God's peace, and it'll be with me. This means that before I send that email, I can pray and discern if it's appropriate. This means that before I post something on social media, I can ask for God's direction. God goes with us wherever we go. We have an amazing resource to communicate in real-time with Him, and He promises to act on behalf of His children.

"Do not be anxious about anything, but in every situation, by prayer and petition, with thanksgiving, present your requests to God. And the peace of God, which transcends all understanding, will guard your hearts and your minds in Christ Jesus." Philippians 4:6–7

Let's stop trusting in our own wisdom and power to solve all of life's problems and realize the fact that for most of what life brings us, we're powerless. We desperately need God.

Abraham Lincoln famously said, "I have been driven many times upon my knees by the overwhelming conviction that I had nowhere else to go. My own wisdom, and that of all about me, seemed insufficient for the day."[53]

Your own wisdom and power are insufficient, too, but God has all of His wisdom and power available for you.

CHALLENGE

REMINDER TO PRAY

Today your challenge is to set up your house in such a way that you're reminded to pray early and often. You could do things like:

1. When you go to bed, put your phone across the room so it's not the first thing you see in the morning.

2. Put new wallpaper on your digital device to remind you to "pray first."

3. Post encouraging notes in the first places you go in your house. Your notes could say things like, "The God of the Universe is near," "God answers prayer," "Prayer works," etc.

How did you remind yourself to pray today?

_____

_____

_____

_____

_____

_____

_____

21/40

DAY 22

HOW YOU SHOULD PRAY

Of the five of the keystone habits Jesus practiced, prioritizing prayer is the most difficult for me.

I want to be better at prayer. I see how central it was in the life of Jesus, and I want it. If any relationship is centered on communication, and prayer is how we communicate with God, I certainly want to be better at it. I know I'm not alone.

Robert Murray M'Cheyne, the great Scottish pastor in the 1800's, once said, "What a man is upon his knees, that he is and no more!"[54]

I'm both inspired and discouraged by this quote. I want to be a man of prayer, but I'm not there yet.

I don't like the man I am on my knees as much as the man who's on a stage. I can boldly and confidently, and even mostly comfortably, preach and pray in front of a large audience. That's easier for me than to be alone with God. When I've preached and prayed in public, I've never stopped in the middle because I've been distracted and forgot what I was doing—no matter how bad the sermon or prayer might have been. But when I pray, distraction seems to be my constant companion.

Truthfully, there have been times in writing this book when I've wondered, "My prayer life isn't what it ought to be. Should I be the one writing about this topic?"

But sometimes we learn the most when we write or teach on a topic, whether we excel at it or not. I like the *New York Times* columnist David Brooks' reason for writing a book on the importance of a transcendent meaning. He "wanted to write his way into a better life."[55] So do I.

So where do we start? I hope you know the answer. It's Jesus.

I mentioned on Day 3 that I was encouraged by the disciples' request that Jesus teach them how to pray. It shows me that prayer can be taught, it can be learned, and it can be an area of growth. When the disciples asked Jesus, He taught them how to pray using what we now know as the Lord's Prayer:

> **"This, then, is how you should pray. "Our Father in heaven, hallowed be your name, your kingdom come, your will be done, on earth as it is in heaven. Give us today our daily bread. And forgive us our debts, as we also have forgiven our debtors. And lead us not into temptation, but deliver us from the evil one.'" Matthew 6:9–13**

I've often wondered if we've gotten the Lord's Prayer more wrong than right. It is one of the most recited statements of all time. Christians have it memorized, and even some non-Christians can recite it word-for-word. However, I don't believe Jesus intended for it to be recited thousands upon thousands of times, especially without thinking about what's being said. He was giving us a model to show us how to pray.

Memorizing the near 70 words of the Lord's Prayer is a profitable practice, but Jesus is giving us more than a rote prayer—it's an example, a jumping off point, for communication with God.

Martin Luther once said: "How many pray the Lord's Prayer several thousand times in the course of a year, and if they were to keep on doing so for a thousand years they would not have tasted nor prayed one iota, one dot, of it. The Lord's Prayer is the greatest martyr on earth. Everybody tortures and abuses it; few take comfort and joy in its proper use."[56]

Jeff Gibbs, one of my seminary professors, echoes this sentiment: "What Christian has not been dismayed by his own indifference to the Lord's Prayer? What believer has not been chagrined when once again she has offered an unthinking parrot-like recitation of this prayer while at the same time mentally reviewing the possible lunch menus when the family returns home from church?"[57]

I want to repeat: there's absolutely nothing wrong with memorizing and reciting the Lord's Prayer, but it was never meant to be a mindless ritual. Instead, it's an exciting invitation to address God as our Father and be in relationship with Him. In fact, I remember as a kid going through confirmation class. *Martin Luther's Small Catechism with Explanation* was an excellent resource to help me learn how to pray through the Lord's Prayer.

For those who know the Lord's Prayer, you might have read the prayer in today's lesson and looked for the words: "For thine is the kingdom, and the power, and the glory, forever and ever. Amen." That's the version I was taught. It was quite a shock for me to learn that scholars tell us these words weren't part of Jesus' original prayer in the earliest manuscripts.

Tradition says Jesus' prayer was so powerful that when a first century scribe was transcribing it, he was so overwhelmed with emotion that he wrote on the side of his manuscript, "For thine is the kingdom, the power, and the glory, forever and

"

WHAT A MAN IS UPON HIS KNEES, THAT HE IS AND NO MORE!

– ROBERT MURRAY M'CHEYNE

#BEINGCHALLENGE

ever. Amen." Then, when other scribes used his work to transcribe their copies of Matthew's Gospel, they thought his addition was the close of Jesus' prayer. That's how the ending of the Lord's Prayer has made it into many of our versions.

This story shows me the power of the Lord's Prayer when we get it right. When we get caught up in the meaning of the words, we overflow with excitement about God, His kingdom, His power, and His glory! The scribe grasped the real meaning of the Lord's Prayer, and his excitement spilled over onto the side of the page. His addition has been the capstone of the prayer for billions since then.

Does the Lord's Prayer do this for you?

CHALLENGE

USE THE LORD'S PRAYER AS A MODEL

Write out the Lord's Prayer today, line by line, and pause after writing each line. As you pause, pray to God in a personal way using the petitions of the Lord's prayer as a guide.

_____

_____

_____

_____

_____

_____

_____

_____

_____

_____

_____

_____

_____

22/40

DAY 23

PRAYER REPS

In the last few years at our church, we've started the year with a special event called "21 Days of Prayer and Fasting." During the three weeks, we hold prayer services every night. Last year I opened many of the services with a five-minute devotion that led into about 10 minutes of singing and worship before we had some quiet time for prayer.

I was always excited about the first 15 minutes of these meetings, but after I finished the devotion and the music stopped, I had a hard time focusing and praying. My mind was very distracted. When the meetings were over, instead of being stimulated and refreshed, I walked away feeling guilty and frustrated.

I felt guilty because if anyone should be praying well at this point in his life, it should be me: a lifelong follower of Jesus and a pastor for almost a decade. I shouldn't be struggling this much to pray.

I felt frustrated because I was genuinely making the commitment and taking the time to instill this habit in a deep, meaningful fashion for our church to start the year, but it didn't inspire me or make me feel closer to God. It's hard to put in the effort when you don't feel the effect right away.

It didn't take me long to realize that both the guilt and the frustration were actually just lies from the enemy. I don't need to feel guilty because the truth is that I'm making strides in my walk with God and in my prayer life, even when I don't sense it. And I don't need to be frustrated because, in fact, when we begin to develop a habit, it often feels awkward, and we don't see much change. That's the thing about habits: you don't always see the growth while you're in the moment. The realization of progress usually comes much later.

The point of prayer is communication with God. We're highlighting many benefits of prayer this week, but the main point is that we get to communicate with God, the Creator and Savior. Through our communication with Him, we grow in our love for Him.

If you aren't sure how to start praying, or you've come to a plateau in your prayer life, I want to encourage you today that the best way to learn to pray is simply by praying.

One of my favorite authors is Malcolm Gladwell. In his book, *Outliers*, he highlights many successful people across many fields and claims they all share a similar characteristic, which he calls "the 10,000-Hour Rule." He considers the rule to be the key to success in any field. It's simply practicing a specific task for a total of 10,000 hours.[58]

Because we're human, it's natural to feel disappointed when we don't see growth. In the gym, I've set goals with my workout partners to hit certain benchmarks. Truthfully, it feels like I experience short seasons of growth and long seasons of being stuck. I love the seasons of growth, and I hate the seasons where I feel stuck. But even when I'm stuck and don't feel like I'm getting stronger, I can look back and see that I've made progress. I need to just keep putting in the reps. As I keep putting in the reps, I'm trusting that the repeated effort will one day help me get stronger.

If you want to become more effective in prayer, simply pray. Put in the reps. You may not notice your growth on a day-to-day basis, but you'll see it eventually.

We like to see change, and we expect to see it immediately. Even the compliments we give people are typically because we've seen them change in a dramatic way. For instance, we compliment an irresponsible person for showing up on time, but we forget to honor the one who always arrives on time. We compliment the person who has lost a lot of weight, but we forget to acknowledge the one who has maintained a healthy body for a long time. I've learned an important lesson: it's more impressive to continue to stay fit than to continually go back and forth in fitness and flabbiness. The nature of putting in the reps is more impressive than big swings, even positive swings.

When you pray, you may not see the direct change in yourself or in those you pray for. You may be discouraged because you don't feel like your prayer life is getting any better. You may not sense God's presence as you pray, but God assures us that He's at work. While feelings are real, they aren't always true. Dallas Willard says, "Feelings are good servants, but they are disastrous masters."[59]

I love that. I'm learning to focus more on truth than my feelings. The truth is that God is always working, whether I feel Him or not. My part in prayer is to continually come to Him, trusting that He's listening to my prayers.

It's wonderful news that God has made a way for us to come to Him. The judgment for our sins has been rendered and the penalty has been paid. We've been redeemed, declared spotless and blameless by the grace of God, so we can come. The writer of Hebrews says that we can confidently approach God. He loves us, so there's nothing to fear. Many of us stop putting in the reps because we're uncertain God loves us and wants to communicate with us. We feel dirty, but the gospel reminds us that we're cleansed by the blood of Christ.

> **"Let us then approach God's throne of grace with confidence, so that we may receive mercy and find grace to help us in our time of need."**
> **Hebrews 4:16**

God doesn't care that much about *how* we come, just *that* we come. We can get so caught up in praying the right way that we lose the joy and expectancy of connecting with a loving and powerful Father. Prayer is an invitation to inhabit God's space. There's not a right or wrong way to pray. Just pray.

In the past, I've used acronyms to guide my prayers. A couple of them are "ACTS: Adoration, Confession, Thanksgiving, Supplication" and "PRAY: Praise, Repent, Ask, Yield." I've used the Lord's Prayer as a model, going through it line by line and pausing, reflecting, and applying it to my current situation. Another thing I've found helpful is praying through the Bible. It's not cheating to pray the words of the Bible. In fact, when I've been in a season when I'm uncertain if I'm praying God's will, the one way I can be confident is using His words.

It's not a crutch to use an acronym, to use the Lord's Prayer as a model, or to pray through the words of the Bible. You may find other tools or models helpful. We can learn some technical aspects of prayer, but we learn to pray by praying.

What's most important is not *how* you pray, but *that* you pray. Put in the reps.

CHALLENGE

PRAY SCRIPTURE TODAY.

One of the best sections of the Bible to pray through is the book of Psalms. The Psalms are a mix of Praise, Petition, and Repentance.

Below is an example of how to pray through Psalm 23:1.

"The Lord is my shepherd, I lack nothing." Psalm 23:1

Praise: If you're having a great day, feeling blessed or thankful for God's provision your prayer could be: "God, thank You for being my Shepherd. In You, I have everything I need."

Petition: If you're feeling like you have needs or you're struggling, your prayer could be: "God, I need You to lead me right now. I'm struggling to hear Your voice in the midst of the chaos." Or, "God, Your word says that I lack nothing, but I feel lacking today in these particular areas . . ."

Repentance: If you're feeling sorrow or guilt for any particular reason, or if you're struggling with living for Jesus, your prayer could be, "God, You are my shepherd, but I haven't followed Your voice. I'm sorry for the times I thought _____, said _____, and did _____. Also, I know You are my great provider, but I still find myself with unhealthy desires. Forgive me, God."

This verse is just one example of how you can pray. Your challenge today is to pray through the entirety of Psalm 23.

"The Lord is my shepherd, I lack nothing. He makes me lie down in green pastures, he leads me beside quiet waters, he refreshes my soul. He guides me along the right paths for his name's sake. Even though I walk through the darkest valley, I will fear no evil, for you are with me; your rod and your staff, they comfort me. You prepare a table before me in the presence of my enemies. You anoint my head with oil; my cup overflows. Surely your goodness and love will follow me all the days of my life, and I will dwell in the house of the Lord forever." Psalm 23:1–6

23/40

DAY 24

PRAISE GOD!

We live in a world of praise, and what people praise is a good indication of the contents of their hearts. To see what people are praising, just glance at social media. You won't be alone. There are almost four billion people on social media across the world.[60]

When I scroll through my social media news feed, it usually contains a lot of photos, including family pictures, vacations, meals, baby or wedding photos, workouts, concerts, sporting events, last night's killer tacos, favorite quotes or verses, and sunsets. When people post these pictures, they're praising these things. People display their highlight reels for everyone to see.

I love what C.S. Lewis says about praise in his book, *A Reflection of the Psalms*: "We delight to praise what we enjoy because the praise not merely expresses but completes the enjoyment."[61]

Praising helps us reach the highest level of enjoyment.

We shouldn't be upset at people celebrating and praising. However, the question must be asked: "What are you praising?" While delicious ribs, sports teams, and cat photos may be praiseworthy to you, there is Someone who is most worthy of praise.

One of the quotes that has stuck with me since my teenage years was John Piper's statement: "God is most glorified in you when you are most satisfied in him."

Are you satisfied in Him? It's easy for us to overlook all the ways God has worked and take Him for granted. In the Bible, we find a story of ten people with leprosy who were healed by Jesus, but only one of them came back to say "Thank you."[62] We often forget to thank God even after He has moved powerfully for us.

A year ago, in January, our church went through our third round of "21 Days of Prayer." As I've mentioned, we gathered on 21 consecutive nights for a prayer service. When we met, we encouraged people to fill out prayer cards. At the end of the 21 days, we sent everyone a list of everything recorded on the prayer cards, and amazingly, not one of them was a praise report or a "thank you." What can explain the lack of gratitude? My guess is that when people were invited to be honest about their concerns, they felt more than a little overwhelmed with the brokenness in their lives and families. Worry crowded out thankfulness.

This observation also showed me that our church needs to practice more gratitude and praise in our relationship with God. As easy as it is to throw my churchgoers under the bus, a church often reflects the heart of its pastor, so I've got nowhere to hide. I need to be far more grateful and praise God for the amazing blessings He gives me. Even when we have critical requests and need God's intervention in a big way, we need to look around and realize how God provides for us all day every day.

A couple of days ago, we dove into the Lord's Prayer. The prayer begins with praise:

"Our Father in Heaven, hallowed be your name."

"Hallowed" isn't a word we use very much, so we need to understand what it means. It means "to make holy or to honor."

Here are two reasons why praising God, affirming that His name is holy, is crucial:

1 PRAISING GOD REMINDS US WHO GOD IS.

In Jesus' time, someone's name wasn't just picked out of a book of baby names or decided because it looked good as a monogram. People's names signified their identity, their family lineage, and a mark of who they were.

When we say, "Hallowed be Your name," we're adoring God's transcendent identity. He doesn't need to be told who He is, but we sure need to be reminded of who He is!

> **"God's name is a place of protection—good people can run there and be safe." Proverbs 18:10 MSG**

The names of God have authority. On some days, I praise God for being the Creator, other days for being my Healer, still others for being my Provider. God's names tell us who He is, what His character is like, and what we can expect from Him.

As C.S. Lewis said, when we declare who God is, we are completing our enjoyment of Him. But there's a second reason to praise:

2 PRAISING GOD ADJUSTS OUR PERSPECTIVE.

In praise we declare who God is, and we recall what God has done, not just in history, but in our own stories. The more I reflect on what God has done before, the

GOD DOESN'T NEED US TO PRAISE HIM. GOD ASKS US TO PRAISE HIM BECAUSE WE NEED IT.

more I praise Him in my current situation. And praise increases my faith: if He has come through before, He can come through again.

God doesn't need us to praise Him. God asks us to praise Him because *we* need it.

As we look at who God is and what He has done for us, by the time we get to our requests, we're looking at them with the proper perspective—the perspective of gratitude and faith.

It's easy for us to become consumed by our problems. Beginning with praise reorients us so that we can look at our struggles, our requests, and even our sins in light of who God is and what He has done.

When you've spent time considering that God has created a universe that's billions of light-years across, how He sent Jesus to be our substitute to die in our place, how He has protected His people, and how every good thing we have comes from Him, by the time we come to Him with our needs, we already have our answer: God is supremely faithful, so we can trust Him.

Our petitions are no longer thrown up in exasperation, in desperation, or with our fingers crossed. We can approach Him confidently, knowing His heart for us as lost sinners, confident in His saving act of redemption on the cross, and believing that He is orchestrating things now for His glory and our growth. He has been, is, and will always be working out His plan for us.

In the opening of the Lord's Prayer, Jesus shows us that God wants to be in relationship with us, and He invites us to pour out our hearts to Him in praise.

CHALLENGE

NAME STUDY

Listed below are Bible verses that contain a particular name or characteristic of God. Read the verses and write out the particular name of God that's used.

GENESIS 16:13 _____

GENESIS 17:1 _____

EXODUS 3:14 _____

PSALM 3:3 _____

PSALM 7:11: _____

PSALM 18:1-2 _____

PSALM 48:14 _____

PSALM 54:4 _____

ISAIAH 9:6 _____

ISAIAH 41:14 _____

ISAIAH 42:5 _____

ISAIAH 42:8 _____

ISAIAH 61:1 _____

JEREMIAH 8:18 _____

MARK 14:36 _____

JOHN 1:29 _____

JOHN 10:11 _____

JOHN 11:25 _____

JOHN 15:1 _____

1 TIMOTHY 6:15 _____

HEBREWS 4:14-16 _____

REVELATION 1:8 _____

REVELATION 5:5 _____

(ANSWER KEY ON PG. 279)

Which name of God do you most resonate with or need for today?

_____

_____

24/40

DAY 25

PRAYERS CHANGES THINGS

One of the questions I'm asked most often is this: "Does prayer change me or does it change God?" The answer is YES!

You benefit from praying. When you pray, you're connecting with God. Being more connected to Him has many upsides: You live with more purpose and direction, and you gain a peace that passes human understanding, a joy that's unspeakable, and even a confidence in the midst of what can feel like chaos. That's a powerful list of how prayer helps us.

But I would argue that prayer also changes God. How is this possible? My seminary professor Dr. Reed Lessing shares this important insight:

> "First, the unchangeable nature of God assures us that we are not in the hands of an unstable force. His promises to Abraham, Isaac, and Jacob [in Genesis, that they will always be His people] form the backbone of the Biblical narrative. This is an 'everlasting covenant.' No one and nothing will separate God's people from His love. God's faithfulness to His people and to His ultimate purposes knows no change. At the same time, we also learn that we are not in the hands of an unfeeling, ironclad deity. Yahweh is a person and as such enters into a real relationship with His creation in which His love compels Him to be responsive to people. Although He must punish those who do not believe, we may rest in the knowledge that we are in a relationship with a compassionate God who is ready and willing to change prior decisions in order to demonstrate His perfect love."[63]

It's a paradox. God's nature is unchanging, but He is unwilling to change in His will, which is to save all people. He longs to forgive those who repent and call on Him, but He isn't stuck or powerless: our God is willing to change His response to people. In other words, He is not unchangeable when He relates to His people! God is at the same time constant in His will, but changing in ways that He interacts with His people.

Can I be honest? I can't fully comprehend the paradox, but when I read through the Bible, one thing is very apparent: when the Bible mentions that God changes His mind, or "relents," it's always for our benefit, not our harm. That's why He appears to change His mind with Moses and the grumbling Israelites, grants King Hezekiah more years of life, and gives the Ninevites another opportunity to repent in the story of Jonah. These examples give us great comfort because they tell us that when we return to Him, He's always willing to accept us back.

What does this mean for us in today's study? It means that our prayers matter! It means they actually make a difference. It means that when we're in conversation with God, we have the ability to affect Him and bring His mercy to people in a lost and broken world.

James 5:16 reminds us, **"The prayer of a righteous person is powerful and effective."** Righteous people's prayers have the ability to change the course of human history.

You may not feel righteous, and in fact, you may feel utterly powerless. But if you're in Christ, you have received His grace and you are declared righteous. You aren't righteous because *you* are good or because your performance has earned the status of righteousness. Quite the opposite. The only way we can be declared righteous is because Christ's righteous life has been credited to us. His death on the cross is credited to us, so we're forgiven, and His perfect life is credited to us, so we're considered righteous. It's all because of Him, not because of us. We have a standing with God that gives us access to the throne room as the King's beloved children, and He loves for us to ask Him for great things. Your prayers can actually change the course of human history . . . and a single life.

I know it's not my power but God's power working through me.

When we believe that God listens to our prayers and they can change the course of history, it means that we can pray with the same desperation that Hezekiah prayed when God granted him 15 more years. We can pray with the same expectation that Elijah prayed when he asked God to send fire down so that others might know that He is the true God. We can pray with the same trust that Daniel prayed when he was thrown into a den of lions. We can pray with the same faith that Jesus prayed with when He healed the sick, calmed the storm, and even raised the dead. We can pray with the same passion that the disciples prayed when they healed the sick, raised the dead, and began the church. And we can pray with the same excitement and hope that our church fathers prayed when they asked God to move powerfully as they advanced the Good News of Jesus Christ throughout the world.

A benefit of prayer is that it gives us direction in a confusing world. But if we really believe what the Bible says about how God interacts with people who pray, here's another important truth: Our prayers can bring direction to a confusing world. Prayer helps not just internally, but externally as well. It changes us, and it changes the world.

Did you ever think that your greatest impact you could make in this world would be through your prayers?

CHALLENGE

THREE BIG PRAYERS

On Day 3, I challenged you with this question: If God answered every prayer request of yours from the past week, what would be different in the world today? Knowing that prayer changes things, write out three BIG prayer requests that you want to see God answer below.

25/40

DAY 26

THE POWER OF PERSISTENCY IN PRAYER

It's important for us to learn one more lesson from a parable Jesus taught. A parable is a story or an illustration that describes a spiritual truth. This particular parable is recorded in Luke 18:1–8:

"Then Jesus told his disciples a parable to show them that they should always pray and not give up. He said: 'In a certain town there was a judge who neither feared God nor cared what people thought. And there was a widow in that town who kept coming to him with the plea, "Grant me justice against my adversary."

'For some time he refused. But finally he said to himself, "Even though I don't fear God or care what people think, yet because this widow keeps bothering me, I will see that she gets justice, so that she won't eventually come and attack me!"'

'And the Lord said, "Listen to what the unjust judge says. And will not God bring about justice for his chosen ones, who cry out to him day and night? Will he keep putting them off? I tell you, he will see that they get justice, and quickly. However, when the Son of Man comes, will he find faith on the earth?"'

This parable stands out to me for three reasons:

First, it's one of the rare cases when Jesus used a negative example to bring out a positive truth about God. He is comparing God to an unjust judge. Why would He do this?

The answer is found in the second reason this parable stands out. This is one of the only times that Jesus gives the point of the parable before He speaks it. The purpose of the illustration is to remind us that we should always pray and never give up. Jesus is teaching us the importance of being persistent in our prayers. He's contrasting an uncaring, unfit, and ungodly judge with a just, loving, and caring God who delights to work on our behalf and give good gifts to His children.

Finally, while most parables leave us with deep thoughts that prompt us to ask a question, this one actually closes with a question: Will Jesus find faith on the earth when He returns?

And to get more personal, let me ask: Will Jesus find faith in you?

Prayer is about connecting with God, but it's not passive; it's an action of faith. Persistent prayer—in other words, praying over and over and over again for the same thing—requires even deeper faith.

Yesterday I closed with the thought that the greatest difference we can make could come through our prayers, but I wonder if there are prayers I've given up on, and if I had continued to plead, ask, and engage with God, He might have answered them.

I have to be careful to avoid treating God like a cosmic vending machine. I don't put in my coin of prayer and automatically expect the answer I want. He's much too wise, and His plans are much more expansive than anything I can imagine. It's not smart to try to box God in.

However, the point of this parable is that it's easy for us to bail out when we don't see the answers we expect. That's Jesus' point in the parable: don't stop praying!

In our culture, it's hard to be persistent in prayer. We live in an instant society. We expect complete and satisfying results, and we expect them instantly. We have drive-thru banking, or even better, we can deposit checks by taking a picture of them with our phones. We have instant meals and drive-thru restaurants and pharmacies.

When I need an answer to a difficult question, I can go to Google and have the answer in seconds. When I was a teenager, I often argued with my friends about sports statistics or who played a certain role in a movie. We might go days or weeks or even months without knowing who was right! Now we ask Siri or Alexa or Google, and we know right away.

When we want to watch a show, Netflix, Amazon Prime, and Hulu have given us platforms to stream the shows. It wasn't that long ago that streaming was just a dream in the minds of some creative entrepreneurs. At the time, we watched a show one night, and then waited a week for the next episode. And we had to endure all the commercials! Now we finish an episode, wait a few seconds, and it's on to the next one. Binge watching at its best!

When I text a friend, I expect to see a text—or at least the text bubbles—immediately.

A few years ago, when we made a purchase, we had to either go to the store or order by phone and wait a week for it to arrive. Now, with Amazon Prime and some grocery and food delivery services, it's not unusual for an order to show up the same day. I've even had something show up 30 minutes after I placed the order. Apparently, Chipotle has utilized drones that can mysteriously come to your dorm room with a burrito made-to-order.

Our cultural expectations have shaped our view of prayer. We pray for something on Monday, and if God hasn't acted by Tuesday, we complain to Him on Wednesday, asking Him why He has forsaken us. By Thursday, we've forgotten all about it. Does this sound familiar?

MONDAY TUESDAY WEDNESDAY THURSDAY

Don't get me wrong. I love all these advances, and I don't want to go back to the days when they weren't available. But with all of this progress, I believe we've lost the art of persistence, because, quite frankly, there aren't many times we need it.

Most of us would do the hard work of prayer if we saw the results right away. We don't mind planting the seed, and we like eating the fruit, but the painful process in the middle—the long period of growth—is necessary for the fruit to grow and ripen. This is the period of persistence, the time when faith is challenged and when faith grows.

Do I have the faith to keep praying even when I don't see God moving? When Jesus returns, will He find faith in me?

Dallas Willard explains, "We don't believe something by merely saying we believe it, or even when we believe that we believe it. We believe something when we act as if it were true."[64]

If you really believe in the power of prayer, you'll pray . . . and you'll keep praying. And as you do, you'll see how God acts on your behalf. That's His promise.

CHALLENGE

THREE PERSISTENT PRAYERS

What's a prayer you've stopped praying? Pray for it again today. Perhaps using yesterday's three BIG prayers as a start, commit to praying for three BIG things over and over again for an extended period of time. It will probably help to post reminders in strategic places.

PRAYER CONTRACT

☐ **I commit to praying for these three things over and over until God answers these prayers for His glory.**

1. _____

   _____

2. _____

   _____

3. _____

   _____

SIGNATURE _____

26/40

KEYSTONE HABIT 4:

SEEK SOLIT

UDE

DAY 27

SEEK GOD FIRST

To kick off the week of solitude, I want to look at the practice of keeping the Sabbath.

A workable American version of Sabbath is that we shut down one day a week. We don't work. We rest, spend time with our families, and give thanks for the work we've completed. I love the concept of practicing the Sabbath . . . except when I pull into Chick-fil-A on a Sunday. When I get irritated that they aren't open, I remember they're following God's commands, and I repent. I reschedule my Spicy Chicken Sandwich combo for another day.

To explore the Sabbath, we go all the way back to the very beginning—the Genesis 1 beginning! By the end of the sixth day, God had created the stars, moon, earth, sky, sea, animals, and the first humans.

> **"God blessed them and said to them, 'Be fruitful and increase in number; fill the earth and subdue it. Rule over the fish in the sea and the birds in the sky and over every living creature that moves on the ground.'"**
> **Genesis 1:28**

Adam had a perfect world, and he had a great job. I bet he was excited and ready to go. The story continues in chapter 2:

"By the seventh day God had finished the work he had been doing; so on the seventh day he rested from all his work. Then God blessed the seventh day and made it holy, because on it he rested from all the work of creating that he had done." Genesis 2:2–3

God's seventh day was Adam's first full day. Adam woke up with a calling, a purpose, and a job God had given to him just the day before.

But God rested. We also know from the Bible that Adam and Eve walked in union with each other and were in perfect relationship with God. What God did, Adam did. I think it's safe to assume that if God rested, so did Adam.

Think about this. God rested on Adam's first full day, and He gave us the principle that we rest before we work. I made the case on Day 4 that God wasn't tired from His work on the seventh day of creation, but Adam wasn't tired either. The Sabbath wasn't instituted because God and Adam were exhausted. It happened when both parties, God and man, were strong and fulfilled.

Adam refreshed and deepened his relationship with God *before* he went to work.

In our culture, we tend to think of ourselves as starting work with a FULL charge. We get up in the morning with a full battery, and we run hard until we're on 1% power, then we rest and recharge.

The Jewish people had a very different daily pattern of life. Their day started at sundown. The first things they did each day was eat and sleep—rest and recharge. After their rest, they got up and went to work.

Their week was ordered in the same way. On Friday evening, as soon as the sun went down, Sabbath began. The first thing they did on Sabbath was eat and then go to bed—not go to worship. That came later. The schedule was very important; it's how God set up their rhythms and habits.

Most people hit the ground running on Monday. We work hard Monday through Friday so we can play hard on the weekend. But our output tends to decline as the week progresses, ending with having fun on Friday night and Saturday, and finally resting on Sunday.

But this isn't how God set it up. Work is not a prerequisite for rest. Rest and solitude first. Then we work.

But we find another important point: Solitude isn't about being completely alone. It's about being alone with God. The practice of the Sabbath is important because it's a time set aside to be alone with God. Many people equate church with Sabbath, but I believe the idea of both Sabbath and solitude, while they include church, is bigger than church.

If you look at the Ten Commandments, only one commandment starts with the word "remember."

"Remember the Sabbath by keeping it holy." Exodus 20:8

We remember something that has already happened, so we can safely assume the practice of keeping the Sabbath had been around for a while. Before God announced the next commandment to Moses, He recounted the creation story

IT'S NOT OUR DOING THAT MATTERS, BUT RATHER, WHAT CHRIST HAS ALREADY DONE FOR US.

when Sabbath was first practiced. It didn't start with Moses and the Israelites at Mt. Sinai; it started with Adam in the Garden on the seventh day of creation.

As we try to incorporate the keystone habits of Jesus, we of course look to Jesus to see how He rested. Jesus' solitude was mentioned nearly 40 times in the Gospels. We see him getting away from people overnight, early in the morning, and even for 40 days prior to His ministry. Did you catch that? Prior . . . not after he had worked and needed to get refilled. He did it first.

All of this points to an important truth about solitude. Solitude has to come first.

Some people feel that because Jesus fulfilled the Law, we no longer need to practice the Sabbath or solitude. But let me ask: What other of the 10 Commandments do we now treat as suggestions? Jesus fulfilled the Law, so that means the Sabbath can be even richer in our times of rest as we slow down our pace. We need to remember that it's not our doing that matters, but rather, what Christ has already done for us.

We have freedom to practice solitude in any way that works for us, but I would argue that it's best to be consistent and intentional.

Solitude isn't just about recharging to get enough energy to get through the week, and it's not just about shutting down work. It's primarily about being in relationship with God and getting to know Him better.

God wants a deep, rich, strong relationship with you. He has the strength you need to accomplish what He's called you to do. Will you meet with Him?

CHALLENGE

TARGET PRACTICE

Assess how you "**SEEK SOLITUDE**" on the target images below. Use these five statements to help you:

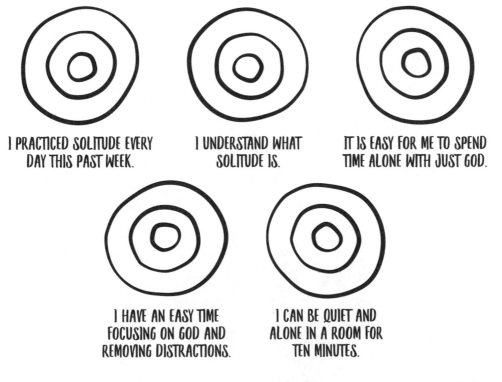

I PRACTICED SOLITUDE EVERY DAY THIS PAST WEEK.

I UNDERSTAND WHAT SOLITUDE IS.

IT IS EASY FOR ME TO SPEND TIME ALONE WITH JUST GOD.

I HAVE AN EASY TIME FOCUSING ON GOD AND REMOVING DISTRACTIONS.

I CAN BE QUIET AND ALONE IN A ROOM FOR TEN MINUTES.

Based on the marked targets, where is your greatest opportunity for growth?

_____

_____

27/40

DAY 28

IS BEING ALONE GOOD?

The definition of solitude is "the state or situation of being alone." But to be honest, I think this secular definition of solitude is actually dangerous. We aren't supposed to be alone. In our prison system, the worst punishment an inmate can suffer is solitary confinement.

A room in Orfield Laboratory in Minneapolis, Minnesota, holds the Guinness World Record for being the "quietest room in the world." Companies often use the room to test products by getting accurate decibel measurements. The room is actually at -9 decibels, so when you get in the room, you can actually hear your heartbeat and the blood flowing through your body. They allow individuals to go in and for tours. Usually, after just a couple of minutes, people start feeling anxious and can't wait to get out. Apparently, the longest anyone has ever been in the room is 45 minutes.[65]

Most of us have a hard time being silent in solitude. Blaise Pascal, a 17th century theologian and mathematician once said: "All of humanity's problems stem from man's inability to sit quietly in a room alone." If that was true in the 1600's, it's even more true for us today! We have a hard time slowing down and finding quiet places, but perhaps at least part of the reason is because we aren't supposed to be alone.

You're made for relationship. You aren't meant to be alone. Ever. It's not good for you. Remember, God created you and wired you for relationship. We already talked about the importance of community, and the most important relationship is with God.

This is important. When we look at Jesus' times of solitude, we see that He didn't get away from all the noise so He could be completely isolated. He got away so that He could be alone with God. For a disciple, solitude is about being alone with God.

When Jesus was in solitude, what was He doing?

He was praying. He went to places that allowed Him to shut out the noise of the world so He could have a conversation with God. And when we draw near to God, He speaks to us. James 4:8 says: **"Come near to God and He will come near to you."** God is approachable, not detached and distant. He loves to be with us, and He promises to invade our presence as we come near to Him.

Solitude is the intentional practice of being alone (or at least quiet) with the purpose of hearing from God. You don't have to book a silent retreat miles away from home or fly to New Zealand's rugged mountains to find solitude.

- Solitude uses your routine shower to create an intentional time of silence and reflection.

- Solitude uses your morning commute and transforms it into a time of prayer.

- Solitude uses your early morning or 20 minutes at night after everyone else in the house is asleep and makes it into a time of journaling.

- Solitude uses an ordinary park bench on your lunch break and turns it into a time of reflection.

Solitude isn't about being isolated. That's dangerous. It's about being with God. And it's a terrific opportunity to connect with Him!

In fact, the only time anyone was ever truly alone was when Jesus Christ was hanging on the cross and cried out to the Father, **"Why have you forsaken me?"** Then Jesus breathed His last. Jesus went through loneliness so that you and I would never be alone.

Solitude reveals your true heart. Archbishop William Temple said, "Your religion is what you do with your solitude."[66] When you're alone, what do you think about? Where do you go? What do you do?

Many of us feel lonely today. We actually spend plenty of time by ourselves, but it's what we do with our alone time that makes all the difference. Spending time without others around is okay, and even healthy. Psychologist Robert Coplan says, "Because there is so much research demonstrating that humans are social creatures who benefit from interacting with others, people will try to dismiss that it's also important to spend time alone. It's hard for them to imagine that you can have both."[67]

In fact, the Rest Test, a huge international study put on by Hubbub, showed that the majority of activities that people believed gave them rest were done alone. The study found this was true for both introverts and extroverts.[68]

I'm sure you spend alone time, but are you spending it focused on worldly concerns or with God? Some of us have gotten so enamored with the things of the world that we've settled for less than the best. Do you crave spending time with God? The early American pastor and author Jonathan Edwards once said, "One aspect of a Christ-enamored heart is a gnawing ache to get alone with him."[69]

JESUS WENT THROUGH LONELINESS SO THAT YOU AND I WOULD NEVER BE ALONE.

When I read statements like that, I feel guilty. My heart cries out, "Yes, I want that!" But often, my thoughts drift to concerns that aren't focused on Christ. When I'm tired, I just want to relax, so I usually turn on the television and watch sports or *Survivor*.

If you look at the arc of my life, you would see that in the big moments and the big decisions, I choose God. But sometimes I have an easier time choosing God in the big decisions than I do in the day-to-day, moment-by-moment choices.

I want to have the psalmist's heart: **"Better is one day in your courts than a thousand elsewhere." Psalm 84:10**

For any relationship to become truly great, there must be time spent together with no distractions.

This is the opportunity God gives us. We get to follow Jesus Christ, make a difference, and be in real relationship with God. Nothing can compare to this incredible privilege. I know this is true in my head and in my heart, and I also know that God gives us grace for the times that our minds and actions are off target. And again, I'm grateful for grace.

CHALLENGE

QUIET TIME

Sit in a room quietly, all alone, for at least 15 minutes, but try to stay longer. Remember that as you're in the room, God is with you.

Keep a timer outside the room and record how long you sit. Mark how long you sat by drawing on the clock below:

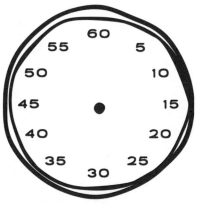

As you thought about God, what things came to mind?

_____

_____

Write down the things you remember from the time alone. Did you feel God's presence with you?

_____

_____

28/40

DAY 29

ANY ROOM LEFT FOR GOD?

Not long ago, I had an opportunity to go to a Brazilian steakhouse. If you haven't been, first, let me just say that while they have a salad bar, it's a vegetarian's nightmare. The highlight of these restaurants is the all-you-can-eat premium cuts of meat.

After you order, the staff brings out slabs of meat, walks around the room, and cuts off slices for you at the table. The way you let them know you want more is to flash a green card which means, "Yes. I'd like to eat another couple of pounds, please." When you're so full you don't think you can walk, you hold up the red card which means, "No more, thanks. Would you get me a forklift so I can get up?" That night, I ordered the premium, deluxe version that had it all. I think I proved beyond any doubt that I'm a carnivore!

First, I went to the salad bar and filled my plate with some extra healthy stuff like salmon, ham, and bacon. Then I came back to the table and enjoyed little Brazilian bread rolls. They were so good! Then the onslaught came.

Several waiters came with the meat: bacon-wrapped chicken, sausage, pork, lamb, duck, turkey, sirloin—just bang, bang, bang, bang. In no time, I was stuffed . . . and somewhat disappointed because I hadn't had the filet yet. That's their top-of-the-line dish. I soon realized these people are smart because they take advantage of your hunger. After you order, they point you to the salad bar, bring out some delicious little breads, and then offer the less expensive cuts of meat. They see your green card and hover over you with platters of meat. It's hard to pace yourself. (Well, I'll speak for me. It was impossible for me to pace myself!)

By the time the filet came, I wasn't even hungry. Here's what happened: I had said "yes" to a lot of good things and had no room left for the best.

When I walked out, I wanted to shout, "Man, I paid a lot of money, but I didn't even get the best they offered!" I vowed to find a different strategy next time I go to a Brazilian steakhouse.

This story is my parable for today, and the meaning is clear: We're saying "yes" to a lot of good things, so we don't have room for the best. And the best is God.

Even good things can become bad things when they take God's place in your heart.

Every day is a battle for our minds. People, companies, clubs, groups, and organizations all fight for our mind space, and we're bombarded with promises and products. Many try to come up with catchy slogans and make sure they become ingrained in our brains . . . and they're incredibly successful.

My question to you is: What are you allowing in? When you hold up your green card, what are you saying "yes" to? And the flip side is: What are you missing because of all the things you're letting in?

As I'm writing this and looking at my phone through the "Screen Time" app, I see that I had 484 notifications on an average day last week. Now, I don't respond every time there's a notification, but that's a lot of dings, buzzes, rings, and pings. Do you think there are more or fewer distractions today than there were ten years ago? Yeah, a lot more.

Distractions inevitably increase unless you take action to limit them. You can set boundaries and limit what you allow in, but distractions are still going to come. Of course, not all distractions are bad. If my wife gets in touch with me in the middle of a meeting and tells me about an emergency, that's a distraction I need to hear. But these aren't my usual distractions. Most of them are articles, emails, and texts that don't require immediate responses.

What are the distractions in your life? And more importantly, what are the distractions keeping you from?

In his book, *How to Lead in a Life of Distraction*, Clay Scroggins says, "Distractions will make the things you want to do in life take longer and cost more than you might realize."[70] College students who change their major 14 times know the truth of Scroggins' observation. It takes them many more years and many more dollars to graduate than the ones who stuck with the same major (or changed only once or twice).

God gives us incredible opportunities, but we can be so distracted that we miss the opportunities right in front of us. If we're not careful, every distraction will become a lost opportunity.

Last week, we saw how prayer brings us direction in a chaotic and confusing world. This week, I want to focus on how solitude can bring focus to a loud and noisy

EVEN GOOD
THINGS CAN
BECOME BAD
THINGS WHEN
THEY TAKE
GOD'S PLACE IN
YOUR HEART.

world. Here's how the two habits of prayer and solitude relate: We can receive direction through prayer, but if distractions cause us to lose focus, we'll miss out on God's best.

The ability to focus comes from spending time in solitude with God.

I want the focus Jesus had, the focus that allowed Him to endure the worst pain and suffering a human could experience on the cross. It would have been easy to be distracted by the voices mocking Him. It would have been easy for Him to react to His body's agony and give up. It must have been tempting to step off the cross, display His awesome power, and start taunting the crowd that was mocking Him. But Jesus did none of this.

Instead, He was so in tune with God that He never wavered.

Jesus offers us a life of almost endless opportunities. The writer of Hebrews tells us that we run our race most effectively when we keep our focus on Jesus:

"And let us run with perseverance the race marked out for us, fixing our eyes on Jesus, the pioneer and perfecter of faith. For the joy set before him he endured the cross, scorning its shame, and sat down at the right hand of the throne of God. Consider him who endured such opposition from sinners, so that you will not grow weary and lose heart."
Hebrews 12:1b–3

CHALLENGE

DISTRACTION CHECK

There are many good things that can fill our hearts, but they can crowd God out of His rightful place as our focus. Below are pictures of good things that could become distractions for us. Circle the top three that are, or could become, distractions for you.

29/40

DAY 30

SOLITUDE'S WEAPON OF MASS DISTRACTION

What do you think these warnings are about?

⚠ WARNING ⚠

CAN NEGATIVELY AFFECT EYESIGHT.

CAN CAUSE CONSTIPATION AND OTHER MEDICAL PROBLEMS DUE TO DECREASED PHYSICAL ACTIVITY.

CAN CAUSE ANXIETY THROUGH INFORMATION OVERLOAD OR OVERSTIMULATION.

RECOGNIZED BY THE MEDICAL COMMUNITY AS ADDICTIVE AND PSYCHOLOGICALLY HARMFUL, MAY ADVERSELY AFFECT SLEEP HABITS.

It appears that the threat is serious . . . very serious . . . almost like a weapon of mass distraction! What is it? If you said smartphones, you would be wrong.

These were warnings against reading books.

For centuries, physicians, poets, philosophers, teachers, and other respected members of the community warned against educating of the masses. However, the rise of the printing press made all kinds of literature available to far more people, enabling them to read in their homes rather than relying on the spoken word for news and entertainment. Some people were fearful of the impact reading would have.

Actually, the skeptics weren't necessarily wrong. Some literature has been used for terrible purposes, but many wonderful things have resulted from the spread of literacy. And today, it's almost impossible to find anyone who is against reading.

When we compare the warnings about books with the warnings about smartphones, we find they're remarkably similar. Although smartphones are a very recent innovation, the feelings people have about them aren't new. And smartphones aren't going away.

THE RISE OF SMARTPHONES

The first iPhone, which revolutionized the industry, was invented just over a decade ago. Steve Jobs said the iPhone was a magical object, and plenty of people agree.

Kevin Roose, a writer at the *New York Times*, observes, "Right here, in my pocket, is a device that can summon food, cars and millions of other consumer goods to my door. I can talk with everyone I've ever met, create and store a photographic record of my entire life, and tap into the entire corpus of human knowledge with a few swipes."[71]

Because of the phone's power and functionality, the way humans interact today is very different from previous generations. Everywhere we go, we see people using their phones—even as people sit around the dinner table. Look at the rise of smartphones in the past few decades.[72]

	LANDLINE PHONES	CELL PHONES	SMARTPHONES
1960	80%	0	0
1980	93%	0	0
1990	95%	.05%	0
2000	93%	62%	35%
2019	39%	96%	81%

According to BankMyCell, the average daily use of smartphones and tablets is 4 hours and 33 minutes, 1 hour and 16 minutes of social media apps, and over 2167 swipes, clicks, or taps on your phone.[73] Ericsson Mobility Report states that in 2016 the average data consumed on smartphones per month was 1.4GB. In 2021, it's estimated that the average user will be 8.9GB of data each month, more than six times the amount from just five years earlier.[74]

According to Asurion, the average person doesn't go more than 10 minutes without checking the phone, in fact, checking it 80 times a day—and the average Millennial is closer to 150 times a day. 63% check their smartphones while using the toilet, and some actually can't go to the bathroom without it! People find it increasingly difficult to pay attention to others because they're so focused on their phones. In the last 20 years, diagnoses for ADHD has nearly doubled.[75]

My point in citing this research is to acknowledge that we're living in a noisy, loud, distracting world. Distraction is our greatest enemy of spending time alone with God.

You might be thinking that with everything I've just mentioned, I'm against the use of smartphones, but that's not the case. A smartphone can become a terrific servant or a terrible master.

It's all in how you use it.

There are significant advantages to a smartphone. Here's just a few:

- I can consume content that will bring me closer to God.

- I can educate myself on nearly anything in a more expedient way.

- I can stay in touch with my friends.

- I can use the device to grow a business or brand.

- I can collaborate with friends or partners without having to be in the same room . . . or even the same country.

- I can download apps that will help hold me accountable as I incorporate the keystone habits of Jesus.

I want to remind you that God isn't against technological advancement. When God destroyed the Tower of Babel in Genesis, it wasn't because He wanted humankind to remain backward. It was because, as Genesis 11:4 points out, the people weren't interested in making God's name great; they were interested in making their own name great.

I don't believe God is interested in destroying cell phone towers. God is always against anyone or anything taking the throne that's meant for Him alone.

A SMARTPHONE CAN BECOME A TERRIFIC SERVANT OR A TERRIBLE MASTER.

But here's the reality: smartphones and other digital devices aren't going away. You—and only you—are responsible for what you let into your mind and heart. And rather than blaming others and being frustrated with the younger generation, we who are adults should ask ourselves: "Is my smartphone a master or servant?"

Technology expert Linda Stone says, "For all the talk about children's screen time, surprisingly little attention is paid to screen use by parents themselves, who now suffer from what's called 'continuous partial attention.'" This condition isn't harming only us; as Stone argues, it's harming our children, too.[76]

If a child were to make a shot on the basketball court and look into the stands and see his dad looking at his cell phone, it sends a loud and clear message that whatever is on the phone is more important than the child. It's one thing to show up to your son's game, but it's another thing to *be fully present*.

It's becoming harder for us to maintain focus in a loud, distracting, noisy world. Many of us need a radical change in our relationship with our digital devices, especially our smartphones. If our devices are always on, how will we ever hear God's voice?

CHALLENGE

POWER OFF

On Day 10, you assessed your screen time. Look again at what you wrote and note if it's higher or lower today than it was when you recorded it that day.

CIRCLE ONE

↑ HIGHER ↑ or ↓ LOWER ↓

The challenge today is to spend at least one hour putting all of your digital devices away. Go for as long as you can today.

How long did you go? How was it?

_____

_____

_____

_____

_____

_____

_____

30/40

DAY 31

FOCUS IS THE NEW SUPERPOWER OF THE 2020'S

One of the major pushbacks against solitude is the assumption that the time we take to be alone will kill our productivity. Some people wear busyness as a badge of honor. Logically, it makes sense that we will accomplish less any time we aren't working, but that logic is flawed.

I have heard it said that focus is the new superpower of the 2020's. Carey Nieuwhof, an expert in leadership, says, "A focused leader is a far more effective leader."[77]

If we look at the life of Jesus, we could argue that He was the most productive human being who ever lived—and Jesus often took time away to be alone with God. How does solitude with God make you more productive? Because when you've spent time with God, His thoughts fill your mind, and you leave with a clearer focus.

We have already seen how prayer can bring direction to a confusing world, but this week's main idea is that solitude brings focus in a loud, distracting world.

If the habit of seeking solitude was important for Jesus, how much more important is it for us who are prone to lose focus?

How does focus increase productivity? Because it helps us distinguish between what's important and what's not. When we don't know what's important, our efforts are scattered, we feel unproductive, and we're not certain what needs our attention. Without focus, we can't be consistently productive.

Earlier, I talked about some of our distractions. The word *distract* means "to draw apart." Its definition is rooted in the two syllables of the word. In Latin the verb *trahere* means "to draw out," or "to have traction," and the prefix *dis* means "away from." Our distractions are drawing us away from something important. Distractions keep us from gaining traction in our lives. Look closely at the word again: *dis – traction.*

A CareerBuilder's 2016 survey found the effect distractions have on productivity: 75% of employers say two or more productive hours a day are lost because employees are distracted, and 43% say at least three hours a day are lost."[78]

That's a lot of lost work hours and a lot of expense. The key is learning how to live with all of the distractions, glitz, and glamour, and yet stay focused on the task God has given us. Ralph Waldo Emerson wrote, "It is easy, in the world, to live after the world's opinion; it is easy, in solitude, to live after your own; but the great man is he who, in the midst of the crowd, keeps with perfect sweetness the independence of solitude."

If our mission is to be greater followers of Jesus Christ, we need to spend consistent time with God to cut through all of life's distractions and regain our focus on Him. Jesus reminds us of the importance of abiding, or remaining, in Him:

> **"I am the true vine, and my Father is the gardener. He cuts off every branch in me that bears no fruit, while every branch that does bear fruit he prunes so that it will be even more fruitful. You are already clean**

because of the word I have spoken to you. Remain in me, as I also remain in you. No branch can bear fruit by itself; it must remain in the vine. Neither can you bear fruit unless you remain in me. I am the vine; you are the branches. If you remain in me and I in you, you will bear much fruit; apart from me you can do nothing." John 15:1–5

The key to productivity is having more of God, not more of you.

By being connected to God in a deep way, fruit will naturally come. When we try to create this fruit in our own efforts, we exhaust ourselves. But when we connect with God by spending time in solitude, we become more fruitful. Solitude is the fertilizer that produces more fruit.

I came to this realization a few years ago after reading this statement: "God can do more in one second than I can do in my entire lifetime." There is a limit of what I can do with my own strength and intellect, but there's no cap on what God can do.

Let me give you an example of how seeking solitude plays out in my life on a consistent, weekly basis. Each week that I preach, which is about 80% of the weeks in a year, I spend around 20 hours getting ready for a 35-minute sermon that I'll preach two or three times that Sunday. My 20 hours of preparation follows this pattern, preferably in this order:

- **MONDAY**: Personal study
- **TUESDAY**: Collaborating with my pastoral team
- **WEDS/THURS**: Writing
- **THURSDAY**: Emailing my sermon to our staff
- **SATURDAY**: Rehearsing my sermon one or two times

GOD CAN DO MORE IN ONE SECOND THAN I CAN DO IN MY ENTIRE LIFETIME.

After all of this preparation, I still wake up early on Sunday morning. I start with a prayer, rehearse my sermon twice more, and then go to the gym to get on an elliptical machine for 45 to 60 minutes. During that time, I worship God and pray for the day. I praise Him for who He is and what I know He'll do that day. Finally, after all the hours of preparation have gone into my sermon, I practice it one more time.

I also find 10 minutes of solitude with God, usually in the shower. I always say something like this: "God, I've done what I can do up to this point. I've worked hard and been faithful to the task You've called me to do. Just tell me clearly: what do the people need to hear?"

I can't tell you how many times in those 10 minutes God has either given me full confidence in what I've already prepared, or He has put something new in my mind. In those few minutes, I experience a peace and confidence that's a gift from God.

It's amazing how important that 10 minutes is for me each week. Your job is probably different from mine, but we're equally called to follow Jesus Christ. If you've been trying to tackle things in your own power and wisdom, let me tell you: give it up, welcome God into your process, and watch how much more He can do.

The key to your productivity is abiding in God, not doubling down on your own strength.

CHALLENGE

SLOW DOWN AND FOCUS

I'm challenging you to intentionally slow down today. Write out the Bible verses in John 15:1–5 (found on pages 205-206), word-for-word. It's a helpful practice in solitude to simply write out Scripture.

_____

_____

_____

_____

_____

_____

_____

_____

_____

_____

_____

_____

31/40

DAY 32

WHISPERS OF GOD

On a particular Monday during my solitude with God, He downloaded an entire worship experience into my head. He led me to change a lot of our regular service. It was a risk, but it turned out to be one of my favorite worship experiences at theCross. We called the series "The Voice of God."

Throughout the series, I taught that God is still speaking. The problem is that we aren't listening. It's not that we *can't* listen to Him, but we're listening to everything else. We probably won't hear God if we don't turn down the volume of all the other sounds around us.

The enemy, the devil, shouts at us so that we hear his voice loudly and clearly, but he shouts from a distance because he doesn't want to come near us. The Bible teaches us that the devil is prowling around like a lion seeking whom he may devour. He's on the move, wanting to shout a quick lie at us and move on to the next person. He doesn't want to be near us, but he wants to be heard so that he leaves a lasting impression.

On that Monday morning, I felt like God told me, "Zach, just tell them that I love them. I forgive them. I choose them. And I'm coming back for them." I didn't hear God's audible voice, but I knew those words were from God.

The title of this particular service was "The Whispers of God." I talked about the reasons God whispers to us, and I declared four whispers over them. These are basic truths, but some of us have been overwhelmed by all the lies of the enemy, so it's important to remember redemptive truths. God is whispering ...

1 "I LOVE YOU."

This is the most basic of the redemptive truths, but we always need its transforming power. The enemy comes to us and shouts, "God could never love a person like you!" But that's not true.

In Jeremiah, God tells us that He loves His people with an everlasting love.[79] In Romans, we learn that God demonstrated His love for us, not when we were perfect and had our lives fully together, but while we were still sinners.[80] His love is an everlasting and unconditional. The love that God has for you is different from any other kind: it's perfect. Jesus loves you.

This is the redemptive truth I hear most often in my solitude with God: "I love you." As a pastor, He wants me to remind people that His love reaches them wherever they go, and nothing can separate them from His love.

2 "I FORGIVE YOU."

For many of us, our lives are filled with guilt and shame—baggage from our past. Many of us have learned to live with it. We wish it would go away, but it hasn't. Some of us are still beating ourselves up over foolish, destructive decisions we've made or current bad habits and addictions that are eating us alive. The voices we heard as children (and maybe as adults) told us we're unloved and unlovable. We feel defective, and we tear ourselves apart. As we condemn ourselves, the devil is right there to kick us even further down.

The truth is that God's grace is big enough to cover your shame and forgive your guilt. The psalmist reminds us, **"As far as the east is from the west, so far has he removed our transgressions from us."**[81]

Rather than continually being beaten down by our sins, the apostle John tells us that when we confess our sins, He forgives us.

I want you to know that Jesus has already forgiven you. Confession is agreeing with God that we've sinned, that He has already forgiven us, and that we trust Him to give us wisdom and strength to make better choices.

3 "I CHOOSE YOU."

It's one thing to be forgiven by God, but many of us still believe our past disqualifies us from being a valuable instrument in the present and the future. What we've done is too horrible, too wrong. God may forgive and use someone else, but not us—we're too far gone. The enemy loves to remind us that we're not qualified. He's not wrong—by ourselves, we're not worthy—but he leaves out the amazing truth that God has qualified us by the blood of Jesus. Our past doesn't have to define our future in God's kingdom. And actually, God often uses the pain from our past to give us new purpose—our greatest impact comes out of our deepest pain.

The truth is that Jesus says, **"You did not choose me, but I chose you, and appointed you to go and bear fruit." John 15:16**

GOD'S **4** WHISPERS:

I LOVE YOU.

I FORGIVE YOU.

I CHOOSE YOU.

I'M COMING
BACK FOR YOU.

④ "I'M COMING BACK FOR YOU."

It's easy to lose hope. We live in a world where the enemy shouts words like cancer, bankruptcy, divorce, terrorism, mass shootings, bulimia, addiction, and abandonment, and we're left wondering, "God, where are You in all of this?" To be honest, I don't know how to answer those questions. But I trust that God's ways and thoughts are higher than ours, and even if I can't fully see the picture right now, I believe that any temporary suffering won't compare to the glory that one day awaits those that believe in Jesus.[82] That's His promise.

Throughout the Scriptures, we see a God who is near to the brokenhearted, the fallen, and those who have lost hope. He reminds us, **"I will never leave you or forsake you." Hebrews 13:5.** Even when you don't feel His presence, you can be sure that He's working in you and for you. He's preparing a place for you. Perhaps you don't hear this whisper often enough because you don't see it happening in your lifetime. The reality is that Jesus could come back at any moment, and when He comes back, it'll be a great day of celebration for all who believe in Him.

This is our future:

> **"I consider that our present sufferings are not worth comparing with the glory that will be revealed in us. For the creation waits in eager expectation for the children of God to be revealed. We know that the whole creation has been groaning as in the pains of childbirth right up to the present time. Not only so, but we ourselves, who have the firstfruits of the Spirit, groan inwardly as we wait eagerly for our adoption to sonship, the redemption of our bodies. For in this hope we were saved."**
> **Romans 8:18–19, 22–24**

CHALLENGE

WHAT DID YOU HEAR?

Which of the four whispers did you need to hear today and why?

_____

_____

_____

Think of someone who needs a word of encouragement. Share one of the four whispers with them.

How did the person respond?

_____

_____

_____

Who else needs to hear God's whisper?

_____

_____

_____

32/40

DAY 33

FILL YOUR MIND

Not long ago, our family went on our first cruise. We had been planning the trip for a long time. I was excited for my kids to experience what many believe is the epitome of worldly joy. There is so much to do . . . and so much to eat!

But it didn't take long after we left port to find out that it's possible to be bored on a cruise ship. More than once, I heard one of my boys say, "Dad, I'm bored. What can I do?"

I felt like those parents at Disney World who spent a fortune on airfare, the hotel, and tickets, but when they finally arrived, the reality didn't match their dreams. Instead, they discovered that Florida is actually really hot and humid, which is extremely unpleasant. And the lines! Oh my, the lines at every ride and show! It becomes a contest to see who complains the most, and it seems they're all in contention! Impatience leads to crying, yelling, and temper tantrums. Disney World is the one place where you can walk 10 miles in a day, sweat four gallons, and still find a way to gain weight because you're hopped up on cotton candy, elephant ears, and Mickey Mouse Ice Cream Sandwiches. Sounds like fun, huh?

I'm pretty sure that every time I've been to Disney World, I've heard parents yell at their children, "Hey! Quit griping about everything. This is fun!"

When my kids told me they were bored, I looked them in the eyes and stated emphatically: "This is fun! If you're bored, it's your own fault!" I gave them a list of activities, including pools, hot tubs, round-the-clock soft serve ice cream, arcade, waterslides, Flow Rider surfing, climbing walls, trampoline jumping, basketball, 24-hour pizza, escape rooms, and I ended with, "What more do you need?"

Their response was, "But Dad, there's no wifi!" As a pastor, I'm so grateful for all the sermon illustrations my children give me!

I believe that what happened on the cruise ship is a microcosm of the world we live in. Many of us, kids and adults, live in fear of being bored. Today, we have a stunning array of options to inform us and entertain us, but the multitude of options seems to paralyze us. There are so many that we can't decide, so the boredom intensifies.

Surprisingly, studies show that when we're bored, we're most creative. One expert commented, "When we are at rest, supposedly doing nothing, our minds have a tendency to wander and our brains are in fact busier when we're not concentrating on a task, than when we are."[83]

Many of us rush through life, always in a hurry. To get to where, we don't know, but we want to get there fast. After his upholsterer noted the unusual patters of wear on the chairs in his waiting room, the late cardiologist Meyer Friedman coined the phrase "hurry sickness" to describe the rushed, worried, preoccupied lives of Americans. The chairs had become worn out along the front of the seat. Anxiously waiting to meet with their cardiologist, people were literally sitting on the edge of their seats.[84]

Busyness isn't the goal. It seems that many of us stay busy because we're afraid of having to think deeply about the big things of life. But for those who follow Jesus, thinking is really important.

A growing number of Christians are exploring the practice of meditation, but some aren't sure about it because it seems so "New Age." Meditation is actually a biblical principle, but the meditation prescribed in the Bible has been hijacked by other Eastern religions. The goal of Eastern meditation is emptying the mind. Biblical meditation fills the mind and the soul with God and His Word.

The apostle Paul wrote the Colossians: **"Set your mind on things above, not on earthly things." Colossians 3:2**

And he wrote the Christians in Philippi: **"Finally, brothers and sisters, whatever is true, whatever is noble, whatever is right, whatever is pure, whatever is lovely, whatever is admirable—if anything is excellent or praiseworthy—think about such things." Philippians 4:8**

In the middle all of the noise, the debates, and the opposition, Jesus found time to spend with God. In His practice of solitude, Jesus was refreshed and renewed. His purpose for getting away is the purpose of Christian meditation: to be filled up by God! It's why He spent 40 days in the wilderness alone before He started his ministry. It's why in the busyness of ministry, He often sneaked away early in the morning or late at night to spend time with God. He wanted to be renewed and filled by the Father's love, strength, and wisdom.

If you're exhausted, you're too busy, and you feel like there's not enough time in the day, do something counterintuitive: slow down and meditate.

Meditation has powerful spiritual benefits and helps in other areas as well. When we look at the benefits, we see why solitude is a keystone habit. After extensive research of over 19,000 meditation studies, John Hopkins University concluded that the practice helps people cope with everything from anxiety and stress to physical pain.[85]

Dan Harris, the author of *10% Happier*, explains:

> *"Meditation, once part of the counterculture, has now fully entered the scientific mainstream. It has been subjected to thousands of studies, suggesting an almost laughably long list of health benefits, including salutary effects on the following:*

- *Major depression*
- *Drug addiction*
- *Binge eating*
- *Smoking cessation*
- *Stress among cancer patients*
- *Loneliness among senior citizens*
- *ADHD*
- *Asthma*
- *Psoriasis*
- *Irritable bowel syndrome"*[86]

The demands of our fast-paced, pressure-packed world can crush us. We can be consumed with worry, and if we're not careful, we can fill our minds with good but secondary things, and we'll try to accomplish our goals in our own strength. But we have a God who loves to fill His children. When we're tired, He can give us the strength to run and not grow weary, to walk and not faint. (Isaiah 40:31)

In the Old Testament, the name of God was so sacred that they didn't write it out. They used only the Hebrew consonants "Yod Hey Vav Hey." Translated to English, it's Y – H – W – H. We then added vowels to make it into Yahweh, which means

Lord. But amazingly, these four consonants are "aspirated consonants," and when spoken together, it's the sound of breathing. So, every time they read the word we know as "Yahweh," they breathed the consonants:

YOD (OUT)   **HEY (IN)**   **VAV (OUT)**   **HEY (IN)**

In every breath, we are literally saying the name of our God. We're declaring that He is God. So, anytime an atheist says, "There's no God," his own breath is declaring that Yahweh is, in fact, God!

CHALLENGE

MEDITATE TODAY

Spend time in meditation today. It's less about the physical pose and more about the posture of your heart. Pick at least one of these three ways:

1 Stop everything, slow down, and breathe the name of God in and out for three minutes.

YOD (OUT) HEY (IN) VAV (OUT) HEY (IN)

2 Stop everything, slow down, and spend three minutes thinking about Philippians 4:8: "Finally, brothers and sisters, whatever is true, whatever is noble, whatever is right, whatever is pure, whatever is lovely, whatever is admirable—if anything is excellent or praiseworthy—think about such things." Think about the following things:

- Something true
- Something pure
- Something excellent
- Something noble
- Something lovely
- Something praiseworthy
- Something right
- Something admirable

3 Stop everything, slow down, and spend three minutes reflecting on any one of these three Bible verses: Jeremiah 29:11, Jeremiah 32:17, or Colossians 1:17. As you meditated, how did God fill your mind? What were your thoughts and your feelings about Him?

33/40

KEYSTONE HABIT 5:

CHOO CHUR

DAY 34

OVER AND OVER AND OVER AGAIN

I didn't see it coming. For years, I was faster, stronger, and more coordinated than my boys, but my son Nathan, only 12 at this writing, now runs faster and farther than me. It's a little thrilling . . . and a bit depressing. At least I still have golf!

But even golf is in the crosshairs because my eight-year-old, Brady, already excels in golf. Actually, he has a more natural swing than mine. On the weekends, I've been taking him to some Orlando tournaments where he competes with other kids his age, and it's amazing to watch these eight-year-olds play. The future of golf in our family is going to be fun to watch!

I wanted to get Brady going in the right direction, so I signed him up for golf lessons. The coach was amazed at how quickly Brady hit through a massive bucket of balls. One of the very first things he did with Brady is slowed him down. He assured Brady that he has a very natural, fluid swing, but he wanted to help him with his pre-shot routine so it could become consistent. Consistency takes practice, so the golf coach asked him to do it over and over again. At first, I was skeptical. Golf lessons aren't cheap, and all this pre-shot instruction didn't seem to be that important. I hoped he would focus on Brady's swing.

But I changed my mind when I read about Jack Nicklaus. In his incredible career, he won 73 tournaments and 18 majors, and a significant factor in his success was the consistency of his pre-shot routine. He was religious about repeating the same mental and physical steps to get fully focused and ready for his next shot.

Jack started behind the ball, then picked out one or two intermediate spots between the ball and the target. As he approached the ball, he lined up his clubface with his intermediate target. He didn't put his feet into position until his clubface was properly squared up. Then he took his stance. From there, he waggled the club and looked at his target, then his eyes went back to his intermediate target, and then back to the golf club and the ball. Then, and only then, he hit the ball.

During one of the most important majors, a psychologist timed Nicklaus on every shot from the moment he pulled a club out of the bag until he hit the ball, and guess what? In each shot, from the first tee to the 18th green, the timing of Jack's routine never varied more than one second!

The psychologist also measured Greg Norman, an amazing Hall-of-Fame golfer, during his unfortunate collapse at the 1996 Masters. Norman went into the final round up by six strokes and ended up losing by five. The psychologist found that his pre-shot routine got faster and faster as the round progressed. Changing his routine threw off his rhythm and ruined his consistency, and he wasn't able to correct it. The moment Norman changed his routine, his performance became unpredictable and his results suffered.[87]

Football placekickers are religious about their pre-kick routines, and pilots go through their preflight checklist. Many other professionals and skilled workers have established clear, repeatable patterns to prepare them for their work. The power of consistency raises the level of their performance.

Darren Hardy, who wrote one of the best books on habits called *Compound Effect,* says, "Consistency is the ultimate key to success, yet it's one of the ultimate pitfalls for people struggling to achieve."[88]

Do you want to see major difference in your life? A radical difference? How does it happen? "Small, smart choices + Consistency + Time = Radical Difference."[89]

Last week I described my meal at the Brazilian steakhouse, and I'm sure I offended some vegetarians. Today, I thought it'd be wise to mention lettuce. Actually, the author of Hebrews talks about "Let us":

> **"Let us consider how we may spur one another on toward love and good deeds, not giving up meeting together, as some are in the habit of doing, but encouraging one another—and all the more as you see the Day approaching." Hebrews 10:24–25**

In the first century when the church was being established, some people concluded they didn't need to go to church. But it's vitally important. These verses encourage us to draw near to God with one another, and collectively hold to the hope we profess.

The author is calling us to consistently join together. Consistency matters.

The earliest description of life in a church is in Luke's history:

> **"They devoted themselves to the apostles' teaching and to fellowship, to the breaking of bread and to prayer. Everyone was filled with awe at the many wonders and signs performed by the apostles. All the believers were together and had everything in common. They sold property and**

SMART CHOICES
+
CHOICES
+
CONSISTENCY
+
TIME

RADICAL
DIFFERENCE

possessions to give to anyone who had need. Every day they continued to meet together in the temple courts. They broke bread in their homes and ate together with glad and sincere hearts, praising God and enjoying the favor of all the people. And the Lord added to their number daily those who were being saved." Acts 2:42–47

This church did a lot of things right, but did you notice their consistency? Luke observed that they gathered together every day.

Unfortunately, by the time the author of Hebrews wrote his letter a few decades later, Christians weren't as consistent in being together to encourage each other. If we fast-forward to today, we find many people that think they can have a solid, growing relationship with God without choosing church.

The modern church looks different than the ones in the first years after Christ ascended. They met daily. Our churches meet once a week, and many people only attend a time or two each month. We need much more than this! We live in a rapid, rabid world that's full of bad news and distractions. It's easy to feel overwhelmed, but more than ever, we need each other. Consistently choosing church will make a lifelong difference for you, for me, and for all of us.

C H A L L E N G E

TARGET PRACTICE

Assess how you "CHOOSE CHURCH" on the target images below. Use these five statements to help you:

I CONSISTENTLY CHOOSE TO ATTEND CHURCH EVERY WEEK.

I OFTEN INVITE OTHERS TO COME TO CHURCH WITH ME.

I USE MY SPIRITUAL GIFT(S) FOR THE BENEFIT OF THE CHURCH.

I'M CONNECTED IN RELATIONSHIP WITH PEOPLE AT MY CHURCH.

I TITHE (GIVE 10% FINANCIALLY) TO MY CHURCH.

Based on the marked targets, where is your greatest opportunity for growth?

_____

_____

34/40

DAY 35

MAGNIFY JESUS

One of the main reasons fewer people are choosing church today is that we can get so caught up in the busyness of "doing church" that we forget why the church exists. It turns out that we aren't the first to make this mistake.

One day when Jesus went to the temple, He was horrified by what He found. Mark tells us:

> "On reaching Jerusalem, Jesus entered the temple courts and began driving out those who were buying and selling there. He overturned the tables of the money changers and the benches of those selling doves, and would not allow anyone to carry merchandise through the temple courts. And as he taught them, he said, 'Is it not written: "My house will be called a house of prayer for all nations"? But you have made it 'a den of robbers.'"

> "The chief priests and the teachers of the law heard this and began looking for a way to kill him, for they feared him, because the whole crowd was amazed at his teaching." Mark 11:15–18

Rather than being a place where the Good News of Jesus was proclaimed, people turned the gathering into an opportunity to make a profit. Whenever the focus of a church is off Jesus and on anyone or anything else, it has lost sight of its purpose.

Many pastors and theologians have articulated the purpose of church, but at its root, the purpose of a church is to bring glory to God.

Jesus told Peter that He would build His church on the fisherman's declaration: "You are the Christ, the Son of the Living God."[90] The church is a group of believers united under that declaration.

The reason the church exists will never change, but other questions—the how, when, where, and who—can be quite varied.

We can look around today and see many different ways church has been organized, and we can take a longer look back in history. Sometimes there's a physical building, and sometimes not. Sometimes there are thousands of people, and sometimes just a few. Sometimes the church uses elaborate stained glass, pictures, artwork, statues, and carvings to tell a story, but people may meet under a tree or gather in someone's living room sitting on the floor. It just wouldn't make sense to have a Gothic cathedral in the middle of a rural Indian village.

The church is a living organism called "the body of Christ," and it has to adapt to serve effectively. Not long ago, the world was turned upside down by the coronavirus. Social distancing forced churches to have virtual services, and we had to stay away from each other. We found creative ways to stay connected, and we stepped out to care for our neighbors. Since the church began, Christians have had to adapt to sudden shocks or long simmering issues in the culture. We must adapt, and we must be relevant, but the purpose still remains the same: magnify Jesus.

Nothing magnifies Jesus as much as when people grow in relationship with Him.

While churches can, and I believe, should look different from one another in many ways, when the assembly of the church is done right, it consistently proclaims the Good News of Jesus Christ. That announcement is what moves people to seek God.

We can't make God move, but we can make room for God to move. By proclaiming the Good News of Jesus over and over and over again, we give the Holy Spirit consistent opportunities to do His saving work, known as *justification*, which brings us into a relationship with God. Justification has two components: the death of Christ is the payment for our sins, and the life of Christ is credited to us, so we're declared righteous. All our sins are forgiven: past, present, and future. Some Bible teachers have said that to be justified means "just as if I'd never sinned." We're justified the moment we receive the grace of God. We're saved by grace, not by anything we can do to earn God's acceptance. Paul explained:

> "FOR IT IS BY GRACE YOU HAVE BEEN SAVED, THROUGH FAITH—AND THIS IS NOT FROM YOURSELVES, IT IS THE GIFT OF GOD—NOT BY WORKS, SO THAT NO ONE CAN BOAST." EPHESIANS 2:8-9

When we enter a relationship with God, we begin a process called *sanctification*, which is a theological term that means spiritual growth. God works in us to change us from the inside out so that we want to please God, and we gradually become more like Jesus. We don't ever move "past the gospel." As we consistently hear the Good News, we're reminded of our sinfulness, both in our past and in our

NOTHING
MAGNIFIES JESUS
AS MUCH AS WHEN
PEOPLE GROW IN
RELATIONSHIP
WITH HIM.

present, and we remember the amazing grace God has poured out on us—and continues to pour out on us.

Gratitude for grace is our motivation for doing good works. It's God's grace and His kindness that leads us to change. We are compelled to live a life of good works—not because we *have to*, but because we *want to*.

Paul continues: **"For we are God's handiwork, created in Christ Jesus to do good works, which God prepared in advance for us to do." Ephesians 2:10**

This book focuses on how the habits of Jesus can become our habits, but we don't do them to prove we're worthy or to earn God's love. We do them because we already have His love, and because He considers us worthy. When we fail (and we will), His grace encourages us to try again.

In justification, we bring our *worst* to God and receive grace. In sanctification, we want to bring our *best* to God to honor the One who loves us. When we fall short, we experience God's grace again.

Responding to the Good News and growing in our faith magnify Jesus.

The church exists to magnify Jesus. It invites us into a relationship with Him and challenges us to take steps of faith and grow in our relationship with God.

CHALLENGE

WHAT'S YOUR STORY?

Just as churches may look very different from one another, our stories are different from one another. Spend some time today thinking about your story, and then write it down—your story is known as a testimony. Describe what your life was like before you trusted Jesus, what brought you to the point of faith, and how your life is different today. As you write, describe the role the church has played in your life, positive or negative.

_____

_____

_____

_____

_____

_____

_____

_____

_____

If the church you attend has played a major role, please share your story with your pastor or another church leader to encourage them.

35/40

DAY 36

SPIRITUAL BUT NOT RELIGIOUS

I enjoy meeting people in our community, but when they find out I'm a pastor, they often tell me, "Hey, Zach, church is okay for some people, but not for me. I don't need it. I'm spiritual, but I'm not religious." They're telling me they're sure they can believe in God and be strong in their faith without being part of a church. If I get to know them better, I often discover they feel burned by a painful past church experience, and they're not willing to try it again.

Church growth experts have seen a very clear trend in church attendance over the past couple of decades. When the trend started, people were considered "regular attenders" if they showed up every Sunday. Later, the term was used to identify those who came three times a month, then two times. Now, most people consider themselves faithful members of a church if they show up once a month. Today, more Americans say they attend services a few times a year (or even less) than those who attend at least monthly.[91]

Almost 40% of U.S. adults who rarely or never attend services claim they practice their faith in other ways.[92] In his book, *Lost and Found*, Ed Stetzer polled young un-churched people and asked them to agree or disagree with the following statement: "I believe I can have a good relationship with God without having to go to church." 90% of those age 20-29 strongly or somewhat agreed, and 88% of age 30-39 strongly or somewhat agreed.[93]

Not surprisingly, as church attendance has declined, the number of non-Christian religions has increased, and the number of "nones"—this term doesn't refer to Catholic women in ministry, but N-O-N-E-S, those who consider themselves to be nonreligious—has grown from 2% in 1948 to 16% in 2007, to 23% by 2015, and it's still rising.[94]

Throughout church history, we've seen opposite problems: some people view the church as their entire life, but others aren't involved in a church community because they don't see it as important. Many people are in the second category, but not because they've made a carefully considered response. They hear claims about the church being a place of love, wisdom, and compassion, but their interactions with Christians have been painful and difficult. Christians, they've concluded, are just as angry, just as mean, and just as selfish as anyone else they know. They call us hypocrites, and to some degree, they're absolutely right . . . at least if we claim to be more noble and kind than we actually are. We need to readily admit that every person in the church is still broken, messy, and fails to a significant degree to represent our amazing God. That's certainly true of me. I've served my church as a lead pastor for nearly a decade, and I have to admit that I've been the reason some people have left our church. I wish it wasn't true, but it is—and it's hard to understand. My conclusion is to advise people to trust God fully and trust Christians wisely.

We *have* hurt one another, we *do* hurt one another, and we *will* hurt one another. The deeper we get into church, the more we will find flawed people with flawed motives.

Even though there will be times that we hurt one another, there are also times we help one another.

A recent New York Times article written by an atheist philosophy professor describes the moment he began to change his feelings and convictions about religion. After he gave a lecture about how monotheism doesn't make any sense scientifically, he was approached by a young man who shared that his older teenage brother had been brutally stabbed to death, and the perpetrator had never been caught. The student explained how his family was shattered. His mother suffered a nervous breakdown and would have been institutionalized if not for her tenacious hope that she will see her slain son again and be reunited with him in heaven, where she was sure his body will be made whole.

These beliefs, along with the consistent love of people in the church she attended after her son's murder, dragged her back from the brink of debilitating sorrow and gave her strength to continue raising her other two children.

The writer goes on to say that to the typical atheist, her belief looks irrational, and therefore unacceptable. But it gave her peace and hope . . . and it was the only thing that worked. The professor observes, "No amount of scientific explanation or sociopolitical theorizing is going to console the mother of the stabbed boy. Bill Nye the Science Guy . . . will not be much help should they decide to drop over and explain the physiology of suffering and the sociology of crime."

This mother found hope in the promises of Scripture, and she found emotional support in her sorrow through hugs, expressions of kindness and compassion, and singing together at church.[95]

I'm not saying that simply going to church solves every problem and will instantaneously make you a greater Christ follower, but it helps.

THE AIM OF A CHURCH IS TO BE A HOSPITAL FOR SINNERS, NOT A HOTEL FOR SAINTS.

I've known many people who have stopped choosing church for a variety of reasons. I can tell you with confidence that I personally have never, ever—not once in my life—seen someone who has stopped choosing church grow dramatically in their relationship with God. Usually, it has the exact opposite effect. I've known many people who were growing in their relationship with God, got "burned" by the church, left, and a year later, their lives have spiraled out of control. It's tragic. This isn't what it was meant to be.

One of the stranger conversations I've ever had happened several years ago when an atheist wanted to talk with me. When we met, he told me about his experience with God and church. He used to be very involved in church, but for a number of reasons, he had stopped going and had abandoned the faith. But he noticed something. When he left the church, he experienced sadness and loneliness. He found that other atheists felt the same way, so they started meeting together. They felt better because they were no longer alone, but they still experienced a significant measure of sadness.

He asked me to give him my opinion of what he should do. I told him to come back to church.

I told him, "Our church certainly isn't perfect. In fact, far from it. There isn't a perfect church. The deeper we get into the life of the church, the more we bump into each other. But we'll continue to pursue Jesus with everything we have. It'll be messy. It'll be sloppy. And the reality is that all of us, including me, are a part of the sloppiness and mess. But we'll forgive one another and see firsthand how God's power is made perfect in our weaknesses. Our church's aim is to be a hospital for sinners rather than a hotel for saints."

CHALLENGE

HOSPITAL OR HOTEL?

Does your church look like a hospital for sinners or a hotel for saints?

List three things you can do to help your church be more of a hospital for sinners or less of a hotel for saints.

 1. _____
_____

 2. _____
_____

 3. _____
_____

36/40

DAY 37

IMMERT FORT: ALWAYS FORWARD

My great-grandpa, Clement Zehnder, also known as Bruder, is remembered as an excellent preacher. The final line of his obituary reads, "He left us with many memories—and also a favorite slogan: *Immer Fort!*" This German slogan means "always forward."

One of my favorite "Immer Fort" stories of the Bible is found in 1 Samuel 13–14.

At this point in their history, the Israelites, God's chosen people, were constantly at war with the Philistines. The Philistine army was so vast and powerful that it caused God's people to cower in fear. Many of them hid in caves and thickets, and an even larger number crossed the Jordan River to escape. By the end of chapter 13, after several raids, the Philistines had captured or destroyed all of Israel's weapons. The only ones who had weapons were King Saul and his son Jonathan.

God had promised victory to the Israelites, but this certainly didn't look like a win! They were hiding or running away, empty-handed, and without hope . . . until Jonathan stepped up. He and his aide sneaked up to the Philistine's camp.

"Jonathan said to his young armor-bearer, 'Come, let's go over to the outpost of those uncircumcised men. Perhaps the Lord will act in our behalf. Nothing can hinder the Lord from saving, whether by many or by few.'" 1 Samuel 14:6

What incredible courage! Jonathan believed that God "perhaps" would give them strength for the two of them to defeat the outpost of Philistine soldiers. There were no guarantees, but Jonathan and his aide were willing to risk their lives for the sake of God's honor. It didn't bother them that they were outnumbered and no reinforcements would come if they got in trouble. It only mattered that God was on their side. Jonathan invited the armor bearer to be a part of the story. The "Immer Fort" spirit of Jonathan was obvious.

Even when the odds are stacked against us, with God on our side, we're able to rise up in confidence, trusting that God will work out all things for His glory!

Jonathan and his armor-bearer made it into Philistine territory and started a battle. These two went all Jack Bauer, James Bond, and Lara Croft on the Philistines, and killed 20 of them right away. The Philistines started to panic . . . at the same time God caused an earthquake!

Jonathan hadn't asked for his father's orders before he engaged the Philistines. In fact, the king didn't know his son was attacking. But when King Saul looked, he noticed that the Philistine army was "melting away" (verse 16) and wondered what was going on. Who was fighting for Israel? He found out it was Jonathan and the armor-bearer. Saul and his 600 men had been hiding, but when they saw the rout, they marched to help Jonathan. When they arrived, here's what they saw:

"Then Saul and all his men assembled and went to the battle. They found the Philistines in total confusion, striking each other with their swords."
1 Samuel 14:20

Imagine the scene: God had shaken the earth, the mighty Philistine army was in panic mode, and they were so confused that they attacked each other! Unbelievable. God was fighting this battle on behalf of the Israelites.

Then look what happened next. There was a third group of people. Jonathan and the armor bearer were the first wave in battle. Saul and his 600 were the second wave. Now, a third wave showed up.

"When all the Israelites who had hidden in the hill country of Ephraim heard that the Philistines were on the run, they joined the battle in hot pursuit." 1 Samuel 4:22

The people who had run away in fear were now running in hot pursuit of the Philistines. I picture them mocking the cowards, when, in just a chapter earlier, they had been the cowards!

All three waves of people saw God do incredible things, and they all experienced the joy and spoils of victory, but I would that argue some got to see more of God's power than others. Think about it. Each wave saw God move, but only two people got to see God move in three ways. Only 600 people got to see God move in two ways. And the thousands only got to see God work one miracle.

We can be in the last crowd, coming out of hiding to taunt a group of people already on the run, or we can have the spirit of Jonathan and the armor bearer who stepped into the promises of God and saw Him do miracle after miracle.

This story reminds me that God is working out a bigger story, and in His story, God wins in the end—and all those who are on His team win in the end. But I don't

IMMERT FORT:

ALWAYS
FORWARD

have to wait until the end to join His story and see Him move in mighty ways. He's inviting me (and you) into His story right now. God will do what He's going to do no matter if we are involved or not, but He graciously invites us to join Him!

If you feel unworthy, it's because you are. But remember, Jesus Christ went up against the most powerful enemy, the devil, against the most powerful weapon the enemy has, sin, and the most powerful result of sin, death, and He conquered all of them. And by conquering them through His death and resurrection, He now offers you the opportunity, through grace, to be a part of the story. It doesn't matter if you are a man or a woman, black, white, or brown, young or old, rich or poor. God says to you, "Receive My grace and be a part of the story." In a world filled with FOMO, the Gospel of Jesus removes this fear. We don't have to miss out. We were outsiders, but He made us insiders. We were disqualified, but He qualified us. We were powerless, but now we have the Holy Spirit living inside us. We had a self-absorbed story, but now our story is part of the greatest story ever told.

God is inviting us into His story, and it's up to us to take steps of faith. Our steps, though, should always be where God has already promised to be. The church has its flaws, but if you want to make a difference and step into His story with the assurance that God is at work, choose church. That's where it happens.

Step into His story—*Immer Fort*, always forward—until we see Jesus return.

CHALLENGE

STEP INTO GOD'S STORY

If you could join God's story anywhere, where would you join and what would you do?

_____

_____

_____

If you're going to step into God's story more fully (or if you've already stepped in), who would you choose to take with you? Explain why.

_____

_____

_____

What obstacles are stopping you from stepping more deeply into God's story?

_____

_____

_____

Reach out to the person you would have by your side and discuss today's reading and challenge.

37/40

DAY 38

A DIFFERENT CHURCH

Not long ago, my wife and I were at a friend's house and played *The Newlywed Game*. The game asks husbands and wives to separately answer questions related to their marriage without their spouse knowing their answer. After all questions have been answered, everyone comes back together, and you have to guess how your spouse answered the question. I'm pretty sure the point of the game is to laugh at the other couples . . . and cause fights among couples who may have felt very good about each other before they walked in that night.

On this particular night, I was asked, "What masculine trait would your wife say that you lack?" Right away, I was thinking, *Surely, my wife will say, 'None.' I'm quite sure that I have every trait my wife would ever desire in a man.* But as I thought about it, I remembered that she has been frustrated with me several times because I've shown that I have absolutely no ability to fix anything around the house. Oh, I try, but I usually end up feeling defeated and frustrated. I'm not even sure if I like Christmas Day anymore because the excitement of opening gifts, which usually last five minutes, is followed by hours of constructing and assembling toys for my children. (That makes me sound awful, and I should probably repent, but at least a few of you understand.)

That night in the game, I wrote "Fixing things." When she came back and was asked the question, she instantly responded, "Fixing things."

For whatever reason, I'm not wired that way. I'm not saying I can't learn, or even that I shouldn't learn, but it's obvious to me that this skill doesn't come naturally, and it's equally obvious that my attempts often cause more frustration than success—for me and everyone in our family.

It wouldn't make sense, then, for me to get a job needing a hammer or a wrench—I still don't know which end to use. God has uniquely gifted me, and it's important for each of us to understand how God has made us so that together we can use our gifts in productive ways.

The church is made up of all different kinds of individuals with a variety of gifts.

To understand how the gifts affect the church, we can look at 1 Corinthians 12. In verse 3, Paul reminds us that the Holy Spirit puts us in the family of God by giving us the faith to say, "Jesus is Lord," and then he explains that the Holy Spirit gives us each a spiritual gift:

> **"A spiritual gift is given to each of us so we can help each other."**
> **1 Corinthians 12:7 NLT**

Paul lists many of the gifts. It's important to note that every one of us has a gift, but no one has all the gifts. Each one is meant to be used for the common good, not so we can brag about ourselves.

Paul describes the church as a body, reminding us that we each play a part.

> **"Just as a body, though one, has many parts, but all its many parts form one body, so it is with Christ." 1 Corinthians 12:12**

Then finally:

"Now you are the body of Christ, and each one of you is a part of it."
1 Corinthians 12:27

In this part of his letter, Paul reminds us that each one of us has a gift the church needs. In fact, the church is incomplete without *all of us* doing our part to extend and deepen the church's impact.

All of us? Even him? Even her? Yes, all of us. We're shortsighted, and we can get too wrapped up in our preferences of what church should look like and who should play particular roles. It's easy to push our agenda as the way the church ought to function. It's fine to have preferences, but we need to realize that God is willing to use people who don't fit into our sometimes-narrow likes and dislikes.

This makes sense because all of us are made differently.

Do you know how God has uniquely gifted you?

I've heard that only 8% of Christians have discovered their spiritual gifts. It's possible to choose church through worship attendance but still feel somewhat disconnected. You were wired to not only consume but to contribute.

In the well-known story of Jesus and the Samaritan woman at the well, we often overlook one aspect of the story: His disciples had left Him alone with the Samaritan woman while they walked into town to get some food. Chick-fil-A was closed on Sunday, so they had to scrounge around for something else. When they returned with their take-out lunches, a conversation began:

"Meanwhile his disciples urged him, 'Rabbi, eat something.' But he said to them, 'I have food to eat that you know nothing about.' Then his disciples said to each other, 'Could someone have brought him food?'" John 4:31-33

They were confused. What's He talking about? Did Jesus have a pizza delivered? Did He have some power bars in the pocket of His robe?

"'My food,' said Jesus, 'is to do the will of him who sent me and to finish his work.'" John 4:34

Jesus explained that caring for the woman and seeing her respond to His love filled Him up more than a great sandwich.

It's really important to fill yourself with the Good News of Jesus by attending worship, but you also take the Good News to share with others. How? By using the gifts God has given to you. Perhaps you've been consuming but you still feel hungry. It's because you weren't just meant to soak up truth; you're also created to share Christ with others. You're a channel of God's truth and grace. Is your channel flowing, or is it dammed up?

The highest level of fulfillment is experienced when "transcendence needs" are met. Nothing is more fulfilling than when we who have achieved our potential serve others so they can achieve theirs.

If church was just about attending on Sunday and receiving God's grace, it would be good, but it would be incomplete. After you've experienced Jesus meeting your needs, you're now inspired to meet the needs of others, which includes those inside and outside your church.

Rather than fighting among ourselves about the "one right way" to do church, let's acknowledge that there isn't just "one right way," and instead, encourage one another to use the unique gifts God has given teach of us as we magnify Jesus together.

CHALLENGE

DISCOVER YOUR GIFTS

Discover what your spiritual gifts are by taking a spiritual gift test. You can find links to spiritual gift tests online at www.beingchallenge.com/gifts.

What are your top three spiritual gifts?

 1 _____

 2 _____

 3 _____

38/40

DAY 39

THE 1 AND THE 111

There are 168 hours of the week. Scientists recommend that we sleep every night for 8 hours—that equates to 56 sleeping hours and 112 waking hours.

It's very easy for pastors and those who attend churches to spend a lot of time, energy, focus, and money on only 1 of those 112 waking hours: the weekly worship service. And we neglect the other 111.

As I've been reflecting on how to lead my own church during the coronavirus pandemic, it's become apparent that the church and its people need to have a clearer focus on both the weekly worship *gathering* (the one hour) and in the *scattering* (the other 111 waking hours).

Part of choosing church and stepping into God's story is committing to worship with a church family for one hour a week, and also, using your spiritual gifts in the other 111 waking hours to build the faith of people in the church and extend its mission in the world.

Yesterday, I introduced spiritual gifts. The gifts are for the benefit of others, not to consume for yourself. If you do nothing with what God has entrusted to you, the church can't become the full expression of love, wisdom, and power God intends it to be.

Jesus attended worship, and He used His gifts there. In all of His temple and synagogue experiences, we see Jesus teaching, leading, and healing (both physically and spiritually). Jesus didn't just show up at church and sit; He used His unique gifts to grow the gathering.

But Jesus also used His gifts outside the walls of the places of worship. Everywhere He went, He taught, healed, and encouraged people. In the supreme gift, He gave His body as a living sacrifice for all of us. He used His gifts for the gathering and also in the scattering.

You're called not just to attend church, but to use your gifts to bless the church.

One of the verses that continually motivates me is the translation of Luke 12:48 that says, **"To whom much is given, much is expected."**

All of us have been entrusted with God's grace, and in addition, the Holy Spirit has given each of us a supernatural ability. God wants us to invest what He has given us, not bury it.

How are you using your gifts to serve others?

Today, I want to broaden your definition of "choosing church" and what it means to worship God. Most of us have thought of worship as what we do for one hour a week, but Paul offers us a broader definition:

> **"Therefore, I urge you, brothers and sisters, in view of God's mercy, to offer your bodies as a living sacrifice, holy and pleasing to God—this is your true and proper worship." Romans 12:1**

Worship doesn't happen only in the 1 hour. It's a mindset of trusting God and being used by God all day every day. Paul mentions a rhythm and an order that's intentional. He tells us that true and proper worship are always the result of experiencing God's mercy. In other words, our part comes after God's part. This is always the order: God first, then us.

WORSHIP FOLLOWS MERCY.

At the time I'm writing this, we're in the middle of the worldwide Covid-19 disruption. It has forced a dramatic difference in the way we do church, but at the same time, it has presented us with new opportunities to spread the Good News of Jesus.

More than ever, we realize that God isn't confined to a building, and neither is His church. His Word, whether it's preached digitally or in person, will continue to accomplish what it sets out to accomplish—changing lives! In the last few months, living rooms have been turned into churches and people are taking more responsibility to be the voice, hands, and feet of Jesus—to people in their churches and in their neighborhoods.

Even when all of our systems have changed, God's mercy remains consistent. I encourage all of us to choose church because we need a consistent rhythm in our lives to receive God's mercy. That's why the gathering, or worship service, will always be important. The mercy that I receive from God, as the Word is preached and my sins are forgiven, is the fuel that I continually need in the other 111 waking hours of the week. Worship isn't limited to the one hour. It can happen in the other 111 too.

The 1 fuels the other 111.

CHALLENGE

WHAT'S MY 111?

List three ways you can use your unique spiritual gifts to serve the church's mission in the other 111 waking hours of the week:

1 _____
_____
_____
_____

2 _____
_____
_____
_____

3 _____
_____
_____
_____

39/40

DAY 40

IF IT BLEEDS, IT LEADS

No matter how you get your news, it's predominantly filled with negative stories. A lot of people feel depressed by the news. Many people believe the media exaggerates the bad news, and they're angry. Still others try their best to avoid the news. Many of us hope the media would cover more positive stories.

Amazingly, a news site in Russia, called *City Reporter*, listened to the complaints, and the producers decided to experiment for a day: They covered only good news on the front page, and they found ways to turn negative stories into positives in the rest of the paper. The results were a lot of sunshine, lollipops, and rainbows—that no one wanted to read! This experiment actually resulted in the paper losing two-thirds of its readers for the day.[96]

We might conclude that people aren't interested in good news. They may not want it, but they desperately need it. In a world filled with bad news, choosing church gives us the opportunity to consistently be around the ultimate Good News—the gospel of Jesus Christ.

The church is where the greatest news of all is consistently proclaimed.

Here's the good news that the church reports:

1 God's faithfulness in our past!

2 God's power in our present!

3 God's hope in our future!

What do you need to hear today?

Do you need to hear how faithful God has been in your past? Hear these words:

> **"When you were dead in your sins and in the uncircumcision of your flesh, God made you alive with Christ. He forgave us all our sins, having canceled the charge of our legal indebtedness, which stood against us and condemned us; he has taken it away, nailing it to the cross. And having disarmed the powers and authorities, he made a public spectacle of them, triumphing over them by the cross." Colossians 2:13-15**

Do you need to hear how powerful God is in our present? Hear these words:

> **"I can do all things through Christ who gives me strength." Philippians 4:13**

Do you need to hear how much hope you have in God for your future? Hear these words:

> **"And I heard a loud voice from the throne saying, 'Look! God's dwelling place is now among the people, and he will dwell with them. They will**

**be his people, and God himself will be with them and be their God. "He will wipe every tear from their eyes. There will be no more death" or mourning or crying or pain, for the old order of things has passed away.'"
Revelation 21:3-4**

Church provides many other benefits, but know this: choosing church consistently puts you in a place to hear the Good News of Jesus!

As I was doing research this week on news, I found an old adage that's still true: If it bleeds, it leads.

In other words, the bloodier, the messier, and the more sensational, the more interested people will be, and then, more will tune in, and the show's ratings will climb.

The greatest news ever read or heard is that Jesus Christ spilled His blood on a cross for our sins. This news is even more sensational because He was an innocent man who died in our place. He took our sin upon Him. The blood that He shed was the payment for our sin so that we can be in right relationship with God.

But this news story wasn't a one-day multiple hour event. It didn't end on that tragic Friday. It turned out to be a full weekend of updates with twists and turns and a shockingly unexpected ending on Sunday morning—Jesus rose from the dead!

Even if Jesus doesn't make many headlines and we don't hear His name on secular newscasts, make no mistake: the resurrection of Jesus is still the leading

CHOOSING CHURCH CONSISTENTLY PUTS YOU IN A PLACE TO HEAR THE GOOD NEWS OF JESUS!

story today. The Good News of Jesus Christ is still causing more ripple effects than any other story that has ever been told in the history of the world!

We have many different options to get news. I'm surprised that many of us keep watching, reading, and listening to such negative reporting. I believe (and as you probably know, I'm not alone) that our world has become increasingly polarized and angry over the last decade. Fury, hate, suspicion, and racism can even creep into the church.

You would think with all of the options, we would choose to fill our lives with good news more often.

Dan Harris, author of *10% Happier*, went on a spiritual journey. He writes, "There is research showing that regular churchgoers tended to be happier, in part because having a sense that the world is infused with meaning and that suffering happens for a reason helped them deal more successfully with life's inevitable humiliations."[97]

If our goal is to faithfully follow Jesus and invite others into that life, we won't succeed if we fill our minds and hearts with harsh, mocking, blaming news. It's hard to tell others about the Good News of Jesus if we aren't consistently receiving it ourselves.

But "If it bleeds, it leads" has another meaning: Let the blood of Jesus and the grace that's consistently proclaimed in churches across the world be the news that leads you to make a difference!

CHALLENGE

SHARE THE NEWS!

Share the Good News of Jesus with someone today. If you're involved in a church, consider inviting someone you know who doesn't regularly choose church to come and sit with you at your church. You could invite them to next Sunday's service, your small group, or a community outreach your church is hosting. The only thing that may be keeping them from coming is the lack of an invitation!

Who did you share the Good News of Jesus with?

_____

_____

_____

Did you invite that person to church?

_____

_____

_____

What was the response?

_____

_____

_____

40/40

THE FINAL CHALLENGE

ONE SMALL HABIT

In my conversations with thousands of people over the years, I've realized that most of those who claim to be disciples of Jesus actually don't have clear spiritual targets. *BEING Challenge* has identified the five keystone habits of Jesus. You can shoot for these, and they will help you grow in your relationship with God.

To that end, I'd like to present one last challenge. Now, after you've worked through this 40-day challenge, I'm asking you to focus on just one of the five keystone habits. It's probably the smallest goal I've ever set for anyone. Pick one—just one—of the habits and set a goal to grow in that habit.

1. COMMIT TO COMMUNITY
2. STUDY SCRIPTURE
3. PRIORITIZE PRAYER
4. SEEK SOLITUDE
5. CHOOSE CHURCH

I've read many books to prepare to write this book. One of my favorites is *Finish* by Jon Acuff. In the first chapter, he drops this amazing statistic: "According to studies, 92 percent of New Year's resolutions fail. Every January, people start with hope and hype, believing that this will be the New Year that does indeed deliver a New You."[98]

Did you get that? *Only 8% finish!*

It's good to start, but it's great to finish, and God has given us the power to finish well. As you clarify your goal to incorporate one habit into your life, I want to give you some helpful advice about making goals and fulfilling them.

1 WRITE IT DOWN

Author Brian Tracy says, "Top people have very clear goals. They know who they are and they know what they want. They write it down and make plans for its accomplishment. Unsuccessful people carry their goals around in their head like marbles rattling around in a can, and we say a goal that is not in writing is merely a fantasy."[99]

Studies back up this premise. A 2016 study by psychology professor at the Dominican University in California discovered that you are "42% more likely to achieve your goals and dreams, simply by writing them down on a regular basis."[100]

Simply writing down your goals will help you achieve greater focus.

BE SPECIFIC

Doctors have always encouraged people to use the outdoors for healing, but usually it was a general directive to "get more exercise," or "try to get outside more often." In July of 2012, San Francisco began two pilot initiatives called Healthy Parks, Healthy People in which doctors wrote actual prescriptions to their patients to walk or run in the park with a set date and time. (The refill line said "unlimited.") It was a joint effort between doctors and park officials to increase patients' time spent outdoors rather than reaching for a bottle of pills. And guess what? A majority of the people actually did it![101]

They found that when the prescription is specific, it's more likely to be followed. This confirmed what Charles Duhigg said of habits: "This is how willpower becomes a habit: by choosing a certain behavior ahead of time, and then following that routine when an inflection point arrives."[102] People have always been told to be active and eat healthier, but they need specifics to turn good intentions into habits: choosing a certain behavior ahead of time and following through to do it.

The more specific you can be with your goal, the better chance you have at creating a habit.

3 SHARE WITH A FRIEND.

We looked at the importance of accountability on Day 12. The likelihood of you accomplishing what you set out to do goes up dramatically if you have a friend who believes in your ability to succeed and will hold you accountable. Just knowing that someone else is counting on you and checking on you increases your chances of finishing what you start.

④ TRACK THE RESULTS

A recent study by Duke University proved what we've known for a long time: when it comes to making plans and setting goals, those who track their results fare the best.

In their study, they monitored groups of people in a weight-loss experiment. They divided the people into groups. One group tracked what they ate on a daily basis through an app, but the other group didn't track what they ate. While both groups lost weight, the one that consistently tracked their weight lost more weight and kept it off.[103] To maximize your chance of succeeding in a new keystone habit, regularly track your results.

⑤ CELEBRATE THE WINS

As you implement a new keystone habit, find ways to reward yourself for progress. There's nothing wrong with rewarding yourself for taking steps forward. When I was an eight-year-old kid, my mom and dad told me they'd give me $40 if I read the whole Bible. Some might scoff at that kind of parenting, but it was a nice reward for someone my age, and it gave me the incentive to read through God's Word, which significantly shaped my young life. It was probably the best $40 they ever spent.

⑥ DON'T GIVE UP AFTER FAILURE

When we fall, it's hard to get back up. Over the years, I've resolved many times to follow a Bible reading plan. I usually start well. That's why my Bible has a lot of highlighted verses in Genesis and Matthew, but I have far fewer notes in Habakkuk and Hebrews. When I missed a day or two, it was easy to miss the next day and the next.

According to Jon Acuff, the day that wrecks goals more than any other is "the day after perfect." He says, "The day after perfect is what separates finishers from starters."[104] He means that if our goal is perfection, we're headed for failure. In fact, Acuff says, "The harder you try to be perfect, the less likely you'll accomplish your goals."[105]

Perfectionism is an implacable enemy of goals. In this 40-day challenge, my goal isn't that you would have accomplished all 40 days perfectly, but that you would begin to think and act on these five keystone habits of Jesus, to realize where you may be weak and strong in your relationship with Him, and develop one new habit that will help you grow in your relationship with Jesus. It's important to have a goal and to stick to a plan, but remember that even in our relationship with Jesus, we're not saved because we execute things perfectly (or even well). We're saved by grace through faith, not by our works. God's grace isn't made perfect through our perfection, but through our weaknesses, failures, and mistakes.

If you're trying hard to apply the truths in the Bible (and in this book), you're almost certainly in a better place today than when you started. When we're in the middle of building a new habit, we're more encouraged when we look back at how far we've already come than when we look ahead at the ultimate (and seemingly unreachable) goal.

If you fail today, it's okay. God has grace for you. He'll pick you back up, and He'll give you tomorrow. And because He's been so good to us, let's give Him our best!

I hope you've enjoyed the 40-day challenge!

CHALLENGE

PICK ONE HABIT

Which keystone habit of Jesus will you improve in?

_____

What goal will you specifically set to grow in this habit?

_____

_____

What friend will you share this goal with?

_____

_____

How will you track the results?

_____

_____

When and how will you celebrate the progress or wins?

_____

_____

Will you commit to not giving up if you fail?

_____

ABOUT THE AUTHOR

Zach Zehnder is a devoted husband, father, 4th generation pastor, author, and speaker. He is the founder of Red Letter Living, LLC and the author of the bestselling *Red Letter Challenge*, which was introduced to the public in 2018. Together Zach and his wife Allison co-wrote with author Doug Peterson *Red Letter Challenge Kids* in July 2019.

Zach met and married his wife, Allison, while completing his undergraduate work at Concordia University Wisconsin in 2004. Zach then graduated with his Masters of Divinity from Concordia Seminary in St. Louis, MO in 2010.

Zach was called to plant theCross Family in Mount Dora, Florida, and continues to lead this innovative and fast-growing church family. Through creative ideas such as breaking a Guinness World Record for the Longest Speech to raise money for a recovery house and paying for the church logo to be tattooed on church members, Zach's ministry endeavors have made international headlines multiple times.

Zach has two sons Nathan and Brady. He loves playing golf with his sons, eating Chipotle, and rooting for Cleveland sports teams! He is a number 8 on the Enneagram, which represents "The Challenger," so it makes sense he would write a book and lead a ministry that is about challenging people to be greater followers of Jesus.

Zach is a highly sought-after speaker. If you are interested in having Zach speak at your church, conference, event, etc. please email hello@redletterchallenge.com or go to www.redletterchallenge.com/zach.

ACKNOWLEDGEMENTS

Being Challenge has been an incredibly collaborative work and I am so thankful for the gifts and talents that many contributed that have brought this book to life!

First off, I simply can't do what I'm able to do without my wife Allison. Her influence is all over this book from beginning to end. She inspires me not just to write, but to "be the real deal." She challenges me to practice the very things I write about and I'm grateful for her support. My sons Nathan and Brady not only provide me with awesome content, but they also inspire me to be the best expression of Jesus that I can be in this world.

I couldn't have finished this project without the help of Andrea Miller. Thank you for caring about the little details and investing who you are into this work!

I'm so grateful for the partnership I have with Steve and Susan Blount and the team at the Quadrivium Group and the incredibly talented team at PlainJoe Studios that have helped bring this idea to fruition!

I'm thankful for more than a dozen friends and family, mostly pastors, that have helped me in creating, reviewing, and supporting Being Challenge. It's a joy to lock arms in ministry with you all!

I'm honored to serve theCross Family as your pastor. I have learned so much from you. Thank you for your love and grace for me.

Thank you all for believing in the vision of challenging everyone to be greater followers of Jesus Christ. I'm truly humbled to know you all!

APPENDIX

What are the most important habits to help us in our relationship with God?

Pastors, scholars, and other church leaders list as many as 30 spiritual habits they recommend to help us grow in our faith. While all of the habits on the list have merit, I believe that *the success of Red Letter Challenge* has been in simplifying and getting down to five easy-to-remember practical targets. My goal for *Being Challenge* was to find the five keystone habits Jesus Christ practiced.

I started with about a dozen different personal or interpersonal habits that we're called to practice. I didn't focus as much on external habits such as serving, giving, and going, which are the fruit of being. These are the ones I listed:

PRAYER

FASTING

SILENCE

SOLITUDE

WORSHIP

SABBATH

SUBMISSION

CONFESSION/SELF-EXAMINATION

CELEBRATION

THANKSGIVING

FELLOWSHIP/COMMUNITY

As I studied each instance when Jesus practiced a particular habit, I was looking for two things: 1) the frequency of how many times a particular habit came up in His life, through either His words or His actions, and 2) specific Bible verses that mention the frequency of how much Jesus practiced a particular habit. As I noticed these habits through His actions or His words, I tracked them in an Excel file.

I admit that I used some liberty in establishing the categories, but the top four were very clear: study, prayer, solitude, and fellowship/community.

As I analyzed the data looking for a fifth habit of Jesus, I noticed a verse that was repeated on different occasions. Matthew 26:55, Luke 19:47, Luke 21:37, Luke 22:53, and John 18:20 all mention the frequency of Jesus teaching at the temple. While numerically, His practice of going to the temple didn't show up in as many verses as the other habits, the content of these verses stood out to me. At certain times in His life, Jesus went to the temple every day. The temple was in Jerusalem, and synagogues were local congregations, similar to our churches today. This is where the fifth habit of Jesus, choosing church, came into the picture.

These five habits are the keystone habits of Jesus Christ, and therefore, ought to be the habits we incorporate into our lives to grow in our relationship with God.

BIBLIO GRAPHY

[1]Kinnaman, David, and Gabe Lyons. *Unchristian: What a New Generation Really Thinks about Christianity—and Why It Matters.* Baker Book House, 2012.

[2]Duhigg, Charles. *The Power of Habit: Why We Do What We Do and How to Change.* Random House Trade Paperbacks, 2014. Pgs. 109-117.

[3]Society for Personality and Social Psychology. "How we form habits, change existing ones." ScienceDaily. ScienceDaily, 8 August 2014. <www.sciencedaily.com/releases/2014/08/140808111931.htm>.

[4]Duhigg, Charles. *The Power of Habit: Why We Do What We Do and How to Change.* Random House Trade Paperbacks, 14. Pg. 17.

[5]"Driving Confessions." *https://www.netquote.com/auto-insurance/auto-insurance-articles/driving-confessions.* Web. 20 March 2020.

[6]Oshin, Mayo. "Keystone Habits: The One Habit that Makes it Easier to Achieve Your Goal." *https://www.mayooshin.com/keystone-habits/.* Web. 20 March 2020.

[7]Duhigg, Charles. *The Power of Habit: Why We Do What We Do and How to Change.* Random House Trade Paperbacks, 2014. Pg. 120.

[8]Clear, James. *Atomic Habits: Tiny Changes, Remarkable Results: an Easy & Proven Way to Build Good Habits & Break Bad Ones.* Avery, an Imprint of Penguin Random House, 2018. Pg. 196

[9]Lewis, C.S. Mere Christianity. Harper Collins, 1952, 2001. Pgs. 174-176.

[10]Polack, Ellie. "New CIGNA Study Reveals Loneliness at Epidemic Levels in America." https://www.cigna.com/newsroom/news-releases/2018/new-cigna-study-reveals-loneliness-at-epidemic-levels-in-america. 01 May 2018. Web. 20 March 2020.

[11]Glaser, Judith E. "Psychology of Deep Connection." *https://www.psychologytoday.com/us/blog/conversational-intelligence/201509/psychology-deep-connection?amp.* 29 Sept 2015. Web. 20 March 2020.

[12]Chalabi, Mona. "How Many Times Does the Average American Move?" https:// fivethirtyeight.com/features/how-many-times-the-average-person-moves/. 29 January 2015. Web. 20 March 2020.

[13]Garber, Megan. "What Does 'Community' Mean?" https://www.theatlantic.com/entertainment/archive/2017/07/what-does-community-mean/532518/. 3 July 2017. Web. 20 March 2020.

[14]Baer, Drake. "If your Best Friend Becomes Obese, You have a 57% Chance of Becoming Obese, Too." *https://www.businessinsider.com/if-your-best-friend-becomes-obese-you-will-too-says-harvard-professor-2014-4.* 9 Apr 2014. Web. 20 March 2020.

[15]"2019 Modern Wealth Survey." *https://www.aboutschwab.com/modernwealth2019.* Web. 20 March 2020.

[16]Mazza, Susan. "Who's in your Inner Circle?" https://randomactsofleadership.com/whos-in-your-inner-circle/. 12 March 2014. Web. 20 March 2020.

[17]Royal, Ken. "What Engaged Employees Do Differently." *https://www.gallup.com/workplace/266822/engaged-employees-differently.aspx.* 14 Sept 2019. Web. 20 March 2020.

[18]Mabiletsa Lerato. "Why Only 2% of People Become Successful." *https://elite-cv.com/blog/why-only-2-of-people-become-successful/.* Web. 20 March 2020.

[19]Westmaas, Reuben. "People Regret the Things They Didn't Do More than the Things They Did." *https://curiosity.com/topics/people-regret-the-things-they-didnt-do-more-than-the-things-they-did-curiosity/.* 2018 May 25. Web. 20 March 2020.

[20]Guinness, Os. *The Call: Finding and Fulfilling the Central Purpose of Your Life.* Thomas Nelson, 2003. Kindle. Loc. 116 of 4496.

[21]Churchill, Winston. "Winston Churchill Quotes." *https://www.goodreads.com/quotes/575705-what-is-the-use-of-living-if-it-be-not.* Web. 20 March 2020.

[22]Newport, Cal. *Digital Minimalism: on Living Better with Less Technology.* Penguin Random House, 2019. Pgs. 104-106.

[23]Twenge, Jean M. "Have Smartphones Destroyed a Generation?" *https://www.theatlantic.com/magazine/archive/2017/09/has-the-smartphone-destroyed-a-generation/534198/.* Sept 2017. Web. 20 March 2020.

[24]Bowerman, Mary. "Survey: Sleeping Together Before a First Date is A-OK, but Cracked Phones are a Put-Off." *https://www.usatoday.com/story/news/nation-now/2017/02/06/sex-before-first-date-intimacy-online-app-dating-sites-match-singles-america-dating-taboos/97341904/.* 6 Feb 2017. Web. 20 March 2020.

[25]Platt, David. *Radical: Taking Back Your Faith from the American Dream.* Multnomah Books, 2010. Pg. 143.

[26]2 Corinthians 12:9-10.

[27]Platt, David. *Radical: Taking Back Your Faith from the American Dream.* Multnomah Books, 2010. Pg. 7.

[28]Clear, James. *Atomic Habits: Tiny Changes, Remarkable Results: an Easy & Proven Way to Build Good Habits & Break Bad Ones.* Avery, an Imprint of Penguin Random House, 2018. Pg. 210.

[29]Graham, Franklin. "My Father, Billy Graham, Avoided Scandal by Being Transparent – and Never Alone with Women." *https://www.nbcnews.com/think/opinion/my-father-billy-graham-avoided-scandal-being-transparent-never-alone-ncna870246.* 1 May 2018. Web. 20 March 2020.

[30]"What Makes A.A. Successful: How to Get the Most out of A.A." *https://www.duffysrehab.com/about/blog/effectiveness-of-aa/.* 4 Nov 2013. Web. 20 March 2020.

[31]Ibid.

[32]Ibid.

[33]Warren, Rick. *The Purpose Driven Life.* Zondervan, 2002. Pg. 188.

[34]Smietana, Bob. "Lifeway Research: Americans are Fond of the Bible, Don't Actually Read it." *https://lifewayresearch.com/2017/04/25/lifeway-research-americans-are-fond-of-the-bible-dont-actually-read-it/.* 25 April 2017. Web. 20 March 2020.

[35]Pennell, Julie. "Here's Why None of us Can Remember Phone Numbers Anymore." *https://www.today.com/money/why-we-cant-remember-phone-numbers-anymore-t29986.* 2 July 2015. Web. 20 March 2020.

[36]Clear, James. *Atomic Habits: Tiny Changes, Remarkable Results: an Easy & Proven Way to Build Good Habits & Break Bad Ones.* Avery, an Imprint of Penguin Random House, 2018. Pg. 36.

[37]Ehrman, Bart. "Bart Ehrman Quotes." *http://www.quotehd.com/quotes/bart-ehrman-quote-theres-not-a-single-scholar-on-the-face-of-the-earth-who-buys-any.* Web. 20 March 2020.

[38]Maher, Bill. "Bill Maher Quotes." *https://www.brainyquote.com/quotes/bill_maher_107546*. Web. 20 March 2020.

[39]Warren, Rick. The Purpose Driven Life. Pg. 192.

[40]"Can You Pass the Test Thomas Edison Gave to His Potential Employees?" https://interestingengineering.com/can-you-pass-test-thomas-edison-gave-potential-employees. 12 April 2017. Web. 20 March 2020.

Answers:
1. 31600 feet at Nero Deep, near Guam.
2. Eli Whitney
3. The Dead Sea at 1300 feet below sea level.
4. Balboa
5. Greenland seems much bigger on the square, flat maps on Mercator's projection, however, Australia is, in fact, three times larger than Greenland.
6. By purchase from France.
7. A statesman, poet, and lawmaker from the ancient city of Athens.

[41]Warren, Rick. *The Purpose Driven Life*, pg. 186.

[42]Smietana, Bob. "Lifeway Research: Americans are Fond of the Bible, Don't Actually Read it." *https://lifewayresearch.com/2017/04/25/lifeway-research-americans-are-fond-of-the-bible-dont-actually-read-it/*. 25 April 2017. Web. 20 March 2020.

[43]Luther, Martin. (1999, c1961). V*ol. 24: Luther's works, vol. 24 : Sermons on the Gospel of St. John: Chapters 14-16* (J. J. Pelikan, H. C. Oswald & H. T. Lehmann, Ed.). Luther's Works. Saint Louis: Concordia Publishing House. Pg 257.

[44]"How Saving Elephants Got One National Geographic Explorer Arrested." *https://blog.nationalgeographic.org/2017/05/09/how-saving-elephants-got-one-national-geographic-explorer-arrested/*. 9 May 2017. Web. 20 March 2020.

[45]Matyszczyk, Chris. GPS Sends Belgian Woman to Croatia, 810 Miles Out of Her Way." *https://www.telegraph.co.uk/news/worldnews/europe/belgium/9798779/GPS-failure-leaves-Belgian-woman-in-Zagreb-two-days-later.html*. 14 January 2013. Web. 20 March 2020.

[46]Cain, Tasha. "Study Says the Average American Hasn't Made New Friend in Half a Decade." *https://www.wtsp.com/article/news/study-says-the-average-american-hasnt-made-a-new-friend-in-half-a-decade/67-61e09c92-ab6d-4d82-a505-056604aa76d9*. 12 May 2019. Web. 20 March 2020.

[47]Fikes, Bradley J. "3 out of 4 Americans are Lonely, Study Says." *https://phys.org/news/2018-12-americans-lonely.html*. 20 Dec 2018. Web. 20 March 2020.

[48]Berger, Sarah. "1 in 10 American say "They'll Be in Debt the Rest of their Lives – Reality is Way Worse." *https://www.cnbc.com/2018/09/05/northwestern-mutual-how-many-americans-say-theyll-always-be-in-debt.html*. 5 Sep 2018. 20 March 2020.

[49]"Living Paycheck to Paycheck is a Way of Life for Majority of U.S. Workers, According to New CareerBuilder Survey." *http://press.careerbuilder.com/2017-08-24-Living-Paycheck-to-Paycheck-is-a-Way-of-Life-for-Majority-of-U-S-Workers-According-to-New-CareerBuilder-Survey*. 24 Aug 2017. Web. 20 March 2020.

[50]Geiger, A.W. and Livingston, Gretchen. "8 Facts about Love and Marriage in America." *https://www.pewresearch.org/fact-tank/2019/02/13/8-facts-about-love-and-marriage/*. 13 Feb 2019. Web. 20 March 2020.

[51]Stepler, Renee. "5 Key Takeaways about Parenting in Changing Times." *https://www.pewresearch.org/fact-tank/2015/12/17/key-takeaways-about-parenting/*. 17 Dec 2015. Web. 20 March 2020.

[52]Clear, James. "The Myth of Multitasking: Why Fewer Priorities Leads to Better Work." *https://jamesclear.com/multitasking-myth*. Web. 20 March 2020.

[53]Lincoln, Abraham. "Abraham Lincoln Quotes." *https://www.goodreads.com/quotes/38057-i-have-been-driven-many-times-upon-my-knees-by*. Web. 20 March 2020.

[54]M'Cheyne, Robert Murray. "Quotes." *http://www.mcheyne.info/quotes/*. Web. 20 March 2020.

[55]Nieuwhof, Carey. "John Mark Comer Podcast." *https://careynieuwhof.com/wp-content/uploads/2020/01/CNLP_316-%E2%80%93With_John-Mark-Comer.pdf*. 18 Jan 2020. Web. 20 March 2020.

[56]Luther, Martin. Vol. 43. *Luther's Works: Devotional Writings II* (J.J. Pelika, H.C. Oswald & H.T. Lehmann, ed.). Philadelphia: Fortress Press. 1999, c1968. Pgs. 210-211.

[57]Gibbs, Jeff A. *Concordia Commentary: Matthew 1:1–11:1*. Concordia Publishing House, 2006. Page 346.

[58]Gladwell, Malcolm. "Complexity and the Ten-Thousand Hour Rule." *https://www.newyorker.com/sports/sporting-scene/complexity-and-the-ten-thousand-hour-rule*. 21 Aug 2013. Web. 20 March 2020.

[59]Willard, Dallas. "Quotes." *https://www.azquotes.com/quote/1226490*. Web. 20 March 2020.

[60]Kemp, Simon. "Digital 2020: 3.8 Billion People Use Social Media." *https://wearesocial.com/blog/2020/01/digital-2020-3-8-billion-people-use-social-media*. 30 Jan 2020. Web. 20 March 2020.

[61]Lewis, C.S. "C.S. Lewis Quotes." *https://www.goodreads.com/quotes/799916-i-think-we-delight-to-praise-what-we-enjoy-because*. Web. 20 March 2020.

[62]Luke 17:11-19

[63]Lessing, Reed R. *Concordia Commentary: Jonah*. Concordia Publishing House, 2007. Page 336.

[64]Willard, Dallas. "Dallas Willard Quotes." *https://www.goodreads.com/quotes/1019974-we-don-t-believe-something-by-merely-saying-we-believe-it*. Web. 20 March 2020.

[65]Scroggins, Clay. *How to Lead in a World of Distraction: Maximizing Your Influence by Turning down the Noise*. Zondervan, 2019. Page 36.

[66]Temple, William. "William Temple Quotes." *https://www.goodreads.com/quotes/7090336-religion-is-what-you-do-with-your-solitude*. Web. 20 March 2020.

[67]Higgs, Micaela. "Why You Should Find Time to be Alone with Yourself." *https://www.goodreads.com/quotes/7090336-religion-is-what-you-do-with-your-solitude*. 28 Oct 2019. Web. 20 March 2020.

[68]Hammond, Claudia. "How Being Alone may be the Key to Rest." *https://www.bbc.com/news/magazine-37444982*. 27 Sept. 2016. Web. 20 March 2020.

[69]Mathis, David. "Get alone with God." *https://www.desiringgod.org/articles/get-alone-with-god*. 11 Jan 2017. Web. 20 March 2020.

[70]Scroggins, Clay. *How to Lead in a World of Distraction: Maximizing Your Influence by Turning down the Noise*. Zondervan, 2019. Page 23.

[71]Roose, Kevin. "Do not Disturb: How I Ditched my Phone and Unbroke my Brain." https://www.nytimes.com/2019/02/23/business/cell-phone-addiction.html. 23 Feb 2019. Web. 20 March 2020.

[72]"Mobile Fact Sheet." *https://www.pewresearch.org/internet/fact-sheet/mobile/*. 12 June 2019. Web. 20 March 2020.

[73]"Smartphone Addiction Facts and Phone Usage Statistics." *https://www.bankmycell.com/blog/smartphone-addiction/*. Web. 20 March 2020.

[74]Heisler, Yoni. "By 2021, the Average Smartphone User Will Plow Through 8.9 GB of Data Per Month. *https://bgr.com/2016/06/02/smartphone-data-usage-2021-gigabytes-erricson/*. 2 June 2016. Web. 20 March 2020.

[75] "Are you Addicted to your Phone?" *https://www.asurion.com/connect/tech-tips/are-you-addicted-to-your-phone/*. Web. 20 March 2020.

[76] Scroggins, Clay. *How to Lead in a World of Distraction: Maximizing Your Influence by Turning down the Noise.* Zondervan, 2019. Page 18.

[77] Nieuwhof, Carey. "5 Disruptive Leadership Trends that will Rule 2020's." *https://careynieuwhof.com/5-disruptive-leadership-trends-that-will-rule-2020/*. Web. 20 March 2020.

[78] "New CareerBuilder Survey Reveals How Much Smartphones Are Sapping Productivity at Work." *https://www.careerbuilder.com/share/aboutus/pressreleasesdetail.aspx?sd=6%2F9%2F2016&id=pr954&ed=12%2F31%2F2016*. 9 June 2016. Web. 20 March 2020.

[79] Jeremiah 31:3

[80] Romans 5:8

[81] Psalm 103:12

[82] Romans 8:18

[83] Hammond, Claudia. "How Being Alone may be the Key to Rest." *https://www.bbc.com/news/magazine-37444982*. 27 Sept. 2016. Web. 20 March 2020.

[84] Ortberg, John. *Eternity Is Now in Session: a Radical Rediscovery of What Jesus Really Taught about Salvation, Eternity, and Getting to the Good Place.* Tyndale Momentum, 2018. Pg. 1.

[85] Foster, Mike. "Guided Meditations." *https://guidedmeditations.mikefoster.tv/?utm_source=ac_email&utm_medium=announce&utm_campaign=guided_meditation&utm_term=1c&utm_content=guided_med*. Web. 20 March 2020.

[86] Harris, Dan. *10% Happier: How I Tamed the Voice in My Head, Reduced Stress without Losing My Edge, and Found Self-Help That Actually Works—a True Story.* Dey St., an Imprint of William Morrow, 2019. Page 168.

[87] Hardy, Darren. *The Compound Effect Multiplying Your Success, One Simple Step at a Time.* Da Capo Press, 2010. Pgs. 100-101.

[88] Ibid. Pg. 5.

[89] Ibid. Pg. 10.

[90] Matthew 16:16

[91] "In U.S., Decline of Christianity Continues at Rapid Pace." *https://www.pewforum.org/2019/10/17/in-u-s-decline-of-christianity-continues-at-rapid-pace/*. 17 October 2019. Web. 20 March 2020.

[92] "Why Americans Go (and Don't Go) to Religious Services." *https://www.pewforum.org/2018/08/01/why-americans-go-to-religious-services/*. 1 Aug 2018. Web. 20 March 2020.

[93] Stetzer, Ed, et al. Lost and Found. B & H Publishing Group, 2014.

[94] Lipka, Michael. "A Closer Look at America's Rapidly Growing Religious 'Nones.'" *https://www.pewresearch.org/fact-tank/2015/05/13/a-closer-look-at-americas-rapidly-growing-religious-nones/*. 13 May 2015. Web. 20 March 2020.

[95] Asma, Stephen T. "What Religion Gives Us (That Science Can't)." *www.newyorktimes.com/2018/06/03/opinion/why-we-need-religions.amp.html*. 3 June 2018. Web. 20 March 2020.

[96] Epstein, Adam. "Here's what Happened when a News Site Only Reported Good News for a Day." *https://qz.com/307214/heres-what-happened-when-a-news-site-only-reported-good-news-for-a-day/*. 5 Dec 2014. Web. 20 March 2020.

[97]Harris, Dan. *10% Happier: How I Tamed the Voice in My Head, Reduced Stress without Losing My Edge, and Found Self-Help That Actually Works—a True Story*. Dey St., an Imprint of William Morrow, 2019. Page 49.

[98]Acuff, Jonathan. *Finish: Give Yourself the Gift of Done*. Portfolio/Penguin, 2018. Page 2.

[99]Hardy, Darren. *The Compound Effect Multiplying Your Success, One Simple Step at a Time*. Da Capo Press, 2010. Page 71.

[100]Morrissey, Mary. "The Power of Writing Down Your Goals and Dreams." *https://www.huffpost.com/entry/the-power-of-writing-down_b_12002348*. 14 Sept 2016. Web. 20 March 2020.

[101]Weinberger, Hannah. "Doctors Prescribing Time Outside." *https://www.outsideonline.com/1803601/doctors-prescribing-time-outside*. 23 May 2014. Web. 20 March 2020.

[102]Duhigg, Charles. *The Power of Habit: Why We Do What We Do and How to Change*. Random House Trade Paperbacks, 2014. Page 146.

[103]"Science News: Tracking Food Leads to Losing Pounds." *https://www.sciencedaily.com/releases/2019/02/190228154839.htm*. 28 Feb 2019. Web. 20 March 2020.

[104]Acuff, Jonathan. *Finish: Give Yourself the Gift of Done*. Portfolio/Penguin, 2018. Pgs. 12-13.

[105]Ibid, Page 16.

Day 24 Challenge Answers:

Genesis 16:13	The God who sees me
Genesis 17:1	Almighty
Exodus 3:14	I am
Psalm 3:3	Shield
Psalm 7:11:	Righteous Judge
Psalm 18:1-2	Strength, Rock, Fortress, Deliverer, Refuge, Shield, Horn of Salvation, Stronghold
Psalm 48:14	Guide
Psalm 54:4	Helper
Isaiah 9:6	Wonderful Counselor, Mighty God, Everlasting Father, Prince of Peace
Isaiah 41:14	Redeemer
Isaiah 42:8	Lord
Isaiah 42:5	Creator
Isaiah 61:1	Sovereign Lord
Jeremiah 8:18	Comforter
Mark 14:36	Abba, Father
John 1:29	Lamb of God
John 10:11	Good Shepherd
John 11:25	Resurrection and Life
John 15:1	The Vine
1 Timothy 6:15	Ruler, King of Kings, Lord of Lords
Hebrews 4:14-15	Great High Priest
Revelation 1:8	Alpha and Omega, Beginning and the End
Revelation 5:5	Lion of Judah

RED LETTER
CHALLENGE

READY TO TAKE ON THE NEXT CHALLENGE?

KIDS

ADULTS + YOUTH

SPANISH

40-DAYS OF PUTTING JESUS' WORDS INTO PRACTICE!

- 40% GROWTH IN SMALL GROUPS
- SMALL GROUP VIDEOS + GUIDES
- SERMON VIDEOS + MANUSCRIPTS

- CHILDREN'S CHURCH CURRICULUM
- SOCIAL MEDIA GRAPHICS PACKAGE
- BULK DISCOUNTS + SWEET SWAG!

→ → → → REDLETTERCHALLENGE.COM/CHURCH